HOW TO COOK
Comfort Food
on a Tight Budget

Catherine Atkinson

foulsham

Capital Point, 33 Bath Road, Slough, Berkshire, SL1 3UF,
England

Foulsham books can be found in all good bookshops and direct from
www.foulsham.com

ISBN: 978-0-572-03748-2

Copyright © 2012 W. Foulsham & Co. Ltd

Cover photograph © James Murphy

A ... for this ... available from the British Library

the moral right of the author has been asserted

Printed and bound by CPI Group (UK) Ltd, Croydon, CRO 4YY

contents

introduction

When you are feeling down, if the weather is cold and miserable or you've had a lousy day at work, there's nothing quite like some good old-fashioned comfort food to cheer you up and reassure you that things aren't so bad after all. Whether it's a warming beef casserole, a wicked chocolate pudding or a crunchy-topped fruit crumble, we all have our own favourites.

These days, we are all having to keep an eye on our budgets, and with this in mind the recipes here are inexpensive to make. Where there are special treats – like the fish pie with prawns – you can easily substitute cheaper ingredients.

And we haven't forgotten that when you need some comfort, the last thing you want is to spend hours slaving over a hot stove, or to find that you need obscure ingredients. So we've assumed that you are fairly new to cooking, and presented everything clearly and simply, including basic instructions on what you need and how to cook simple, healthy food.

- You don't need any fancy equipment – everything will be found in a basic kitchen.

- The ingredients are all readily available – plus we'll help you to build up a store cupboard so you can rustle up a meal or a treat at a moment's notice.

- There's no fancy jargon to confuse you.

- We've minimised weighing and measuring.

- All the methods are presented step by step, so even beginners will end up with a tasty, wholesome meal.

- Most of the recipes are designed for two, but they are easy to double up if you are cooking for more.

Our Menu

Browse Our Menu

You'll be sure to find something to suit your mood. It's all cooked so simply that the effort won't get in the way of your enjoyment.

Our Menu

Soup meals

Minestrone
The classic Italian 'big soup' made simple but delicious with bacon, beans and vegetables in a pesto-flavoured stock sprinkled with Parmesan. *p30*

Main meal mulligatawny
Thick and gently spicy, the chicken, carrot, celery and tomatoes complement the apple chunks and curry flavouring. *p32*

French onion soup
Golden-toasted cheese on a baguette floats in this classic rich caramelised onion soup, delicately flavoured with white wine. *p34*

Creamy chicken and corn chowder
This rich and thick chicken and sweetcorn soup is made with milk and tasty chicken stock and flavoured with herbs. *p36*

Quick vegetable soup
With the vegetable combination you like best, this lightly creamed soup is delicately flavoured with mixed herbs. *p38*

Traditional chicken noodle soup
The ultimate comfort food, this warming recipe is a deliciously simple way to remind you of mum's cooking. *p40*

Sausages and bacon

Sausage cassoulet
A simple version of the classic, use your favourite
sausages in this bean-topped, onion and garlic-
flavoured casserole. *p42*

Spicy sausage pasta
Spicy fried sausages nestling in penne pasta smothered
in an onion, herb and garlic-flavoured tomato sauce. *p44*

Pasta carbonara
Crispy bacon pieces subtly flavoured with garlic
dotted through a creamy egg and Parmesan sauce
swaddling *al dente* tagliatelle. *p46*

Broccoli and cauliflower cheese
Fresh broccoli and cauliflower florets in a Dijon-mustard
spiked cheese sauce and served with a tomato salad. *p48*

Toad in the hole
Thick, golden pork sausages cuddled in a blanket
of golden-brown Yorkshire pudding –
comfort food at its best. *p50*

Mince

Chilli con carne
The Mexican favourite of chilli-spiced minced beef
and kidney beans in a tomato sauce flavoured
with dark sugar and herbs. *p52*

Cottage pie
The classic comfort food to remind you of
home cooking, with a tasty beef and vegetable layer
topped with creamy, buttered mashed potato. *p54*

Lamb kofte kebabs

The spicy mix of garlic, ginger and chilli infuse these meatballs, nestling in warm pittas with coriander-flavoured yoghurt and fresh lettuce. *p56*

Spaghetti Bolognese

A favourite dish that needs little introduction, vegetables and minced beef with tomatoes, wine and herbs create a simple classic. *p58*

Beef and pepper linguine

Thick ribbons of perfectly soft pasta cooked with mince and green peppers and seasoned with onion and soy flavours. *p60*

Beef

Beef and mushroom noodles

A delicious oriental dish, slivers of beef combine with broccoli, mushrooms and spring onions in a soy-flavoured sauce. *p62*

Beef in beer

An old-fashioned stew that gently simmers beef and onions in rich beef stock for the tenderest meat and great flavour. *p64*

Beef goulash

The classic Hungarian dish, steak and vegetables are laced with paprika and cooked until tender in a herb-flavoured tomato sauce. *p66*

Steak and mushroom pie

An old English classic made easy with ready-rolled puff pastry on top of beef and mushrooms in a rich gravy. *p68*

Steak with shallots and wine
Deliciously tender beef steaks quickly seared, then gently coated in softly fried shallots and red wine. *p70*

Lamb

Moroccan lamb with couscous
The sweet element of North African cuisine is represented by the apricots cooked with lamb and spices to a delicious finish. *p72*

Lancashire hot-pot
Rich and filling, this traditional dish from northern England combines lamb, potatoes and vegetables in a tasty gravy. *p74*

Oven-baked lamb biryani
A delicious curry in which the rice is cooked with lamb, mushrooms and peas to impart the Indian flavours through the whole dish. *p76*

Lamb rogan josh
A classic lamb curry no less tasty for being quick and easy to make and serve with naan bread. *p78*

Pork

Sticky spare ribs
The classic sweet-and-sour flavours of garlic, honey, wine vinegar and mustard create a tasty, sticky glaze on tender spare ribs. *p80*

Gammon with pineapple relish
Another comforting retro favourite, a sweet and sour pineapple relish complements generous slices of grilled gammon. *p82*

Oven-roast pork with honey and mustard
A delicious sticky-sweet glaze coats thin slices of
oven-roast pork tenderloin. *p84*

Herb and onion pork
Foil parcels seal in the flavour and succulence of
pork chops topped with onion, apple and potatoes
with a sprinkling of mixed herbs. *p86*

Chicken

One-pot chicken
Your whole meal in one pan, chicken strips are
simmered with onion, potatoes, tomatoes and pepper
in a herbed chicken stock. *p88*

Simple Sunday roast
Classic roast chicken, potatoes and vegetables –
this traditional Sunday dish makes a great meal
any day of the week. *p90*

Cajun chicken and oven-cooked rice
Cajun seasoning bakes to a spicy coating on chicken
fillets served with rice and red kidney beans. *p92*

Thai green chicken curry
Coconut, ginger and lemon grass are the signature
flavours of this mild curry with chicken, sweetcorn
and bamboo shoots. *p94*

Creamy chicken korma
So many people's favourite curry, this is a delicious
version of this mild but tasty chicken dish. *p96*

Honey-glazed chicken
An orange-flavoured, slightly sweet glaze gives a
delicious finish to these tender strips of chicken. *p98*

Creamy mushroom chicken

The name says it all – a simple dish, quick to make but with bags of flavour. *p100*

Turkey

Stir-fry turkey with noodles

The tang of ginger, soy sauce and lemon impart their oriental flavours to a stir-fry of turkey and crisp vegetables. *p102*

Turkey satay sticks

Grilled turkey kebabs with a deliciously sweet chilli-flavoured peanut dipping sauce on the side. *p104*

Pan-fried turkey escalopes

Golden brown with the delicate crunch of breadcrumbs and flavour of fresh butter, these make a delicious easy supper. *p106*

Fish and seafood

Fish and vegetable parcels

Release the aromas of fish, leek, mushrooms and carrots, with a subtle hint of lemon, when you open your baked parcel. *p108*

Tasty tuna fishcakes

Fishcakes are brilliant comfort foods and these use tuna and potato flavoured with pesto and coated in polenta. *p110*

Citrus salmon with stir-fried vegetables

The sharp tang of lemon is the ideal foil for rich salmon steaks resting on top of a pile of crisp stir-fried vegetables. *p112*

Creamy fish pie

A wonderful memory of childhood, fish and prawns
in a tasty, creamy white sauce topped with lightly
seasoned, buttery mashed potato. *p114*

Seafood paella

A simple version of this classic Spanish dish
combines seafood, rice and vegetables in a herbed
and lightly spicy sauce. *p116*

Prawn and cashew stir-fry

A take-away favourite, prawns and nuts go perfectly
with the soy, orange and honey sauce. *p118*

Thai crab cakes

Lightly spiced with chilli and lemon, delicate crabmeat
is coated in breadcrumbs and shallow-fried to a
golden coating. *p120*

Spicy seafood pasta

A simple dish that's great for after work, mixed seafood,
spring onions and chunky pasta are cooked in a mildly
chilli-spiced sauce. *p122*

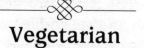

Vegetarian

Spicy vegetable and pasta bake

Mediterranean vegetables nestle with *al dente* pasta
shapes in a rich tomato and herb sauce. *p124*

Vegetable crumble

A new, savoury twist on an old favourite, a crunchy
cheese and nut topping hides a layer of delicious
fresh vegetables. *p126*

Filo-topped vegetable pie

Your favourite vegetables bathed in a creamy herb sauce
with a topping of crumpled, golden-baked filo pastry. *p128*

Potato and pea frittata

Spanish-inspired, chunks of potato are set in a deep herb and cheese omelette – perfect for that taste-of-home-comforts lunch box. *p130*

Cheese and courgette tart

Courgette slices, onions and cherry tomatoes baked with a golden mozzarella topping in a crisp pastry case. *p132*

Cheese and bread pudding

Bread slices are interspersed with grated cheese, soaked in seasoned egg and milk and baked until golden on top and soft beneath. *p134*

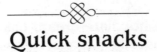

Quick snacks

Salmon-stuffed jacket potatoes

Flaked salmon with yoghurt and cream cheese melting over a soft, fluffy potato. *p136*

One-pot chicken noodles

Stir-fried chicken chunks with spring onions and peppers, seasoned with soy sauce and garlic and stirred into soft egg noodles. *p138*

Easy egg-fried rice

Everyone's favourite quick accompaniment of rice fried up with peas, pepper, corn and a dash of soy sauce. *p140*

Potato wedges and cheese dip

Chunky wedges of jacket potato oven-crisped until dark golden, then dunked in soured cream, mustard and tomato dip. *p142*

Nachos

Cheddar-drizzled corn chips flashed under a hot grill and served with spicy tomato salsa. *p144*

Sweet stuff

Gooey chocolate pudding
A crisp topping and meltingly soft centre makes this rich chocolate dessert the ultimate comfort food. *p146*

Crunchy oat fruit crumble
Oats mixed into the crumble give it extra flavour and crunch to contrast the soft fruit beneath. *p148*

Golden double syrup pudding
With lashings of warm syrup and swathed in creamy custard, if this light pudding doesn't bring comfort, nothing will! *p150*

Chocolate cream cake
Always moist and richly chocolate-flavoured, and bulging cream, this slices neatly for teatime or dessert. *p152*

Chocolate chip cookies
A must-have in a book on comfort food, these delicious chocolate-chip biscuits have just the right combination of crunch and melt. *p154*

Blueberry and white chocolate muffins
Light and aromatic, dotted with juicy fruit and melting white chocolate – can you resist? *p156*

what you need

If you are new to cooking and not sure what you need to buy, keep it to the minimum and add items as you need them. If you have these basics – plus crockery, cutlery, tea towels and washing up cloths – you'll be fine.

Don't bother with gadgets – many are a waste of space. I have listed an electric hand whisk and an electric hand blender as useful options, both of which are cheap, versatile and very handy. If you like the look of something more fancy, see if you can borrow one before you buy.

basic essentials
- Casserole dish – Pyrex is multi-functional
- Chopping board
- Colander or large sieve for straining vegetables
- Fish slice for lifting foods out of a frying pan
- Frying pan
- Grater
- Mug for measuring
- Oven gloves
- Roasting tins
- Saucepans with lids – ideally, small, medium and large
- Sharp knife
- Tablespoon
- Teaspoon
- Wooden spoon

useful but not essential
- Draining spoon
- Electric hand blender
- Electric hand whisk
- Measuring spoons
- Potato masher (use a fork if you don't have one)
- Potato peeler (easier than a vegetable knife)
- Whisk (again, use a fork if you don't have one)

in your cupboard

If you have a few things in the cupboard, you can always throw something together at the last minute. Here's a list of useful basics as a starter for ten.

keep in the cupboard (or the fridge/freezer)

- Baked beans
- Bread
- Butter or margarine
- Cheddar or other hard cheese
- Chilli powder
- Couscous
- Cornflour (cornstarch)
- Curry paste or powder
- Eggs
- Garlic – a tub of chopped or a tube of garlic paste
- Ginger – a tub of chopped or tube of ginger paste
- Herbs – dried mixed
- Honey
- Lemon juice
- Mayonnaise or salad cream
- Milk
- Oil
- Pasta
- Plain (all-purpose) flour
- Polenta
- Red kidney beans
- Rice – long-grain
- Salt and freshly ground black pepper
- Soy sauce
- Stock cubes
- Sugar
- Tea and coffee
- Tomato ketchup (catsup)
- Tomato purée (paste)
- Tomatoes, canned
- Tuna
- Vinegar
- Worcestershire sauce

keeping it fresh

Use your common sense here and keep an eye on the labelling – it's there to stop you getting a nasty stomach upset – or worse – and no-one wants that.

- Sell-by date means you have a few days to use it up.
- Use-by date means just that.
- Best before means you should ideally use it by then but you usually have a few more days.
- Keep all these in the fridge:
    raw meat for 1–2 days
    cooked meat for 2–3 days
    eggs until their best-before date
    cheese for 2 weeks
    salad stuff for 1 week
- Wrap things well in cling film to store them in the fridge.
- Keep raw meats at the bottom where they won't drip on anything.
- Don't put opened cans in the fridge. Transfer the food to a plastic tub or bowl.
- Keep these in a cool, dark place:
    potatoes for 1–2 weeks
    onions for ages
    carrots for 4–5 days
    parsnips for 4–5 days
- Your nose is a good guide – if it smells off, chances are it is off.
- If it's mouldy, throw it out.
- If potatoes are green, throw them out.
- Thaw frozen foods thoroughly before you cook them, unless it's something like fish fingers or frozen peas.
- Don't refreeze anything.
- Don't leave cooked food lying around.
- If you reheat food, make sure it is piping hot right through.

cooking tips

All recipe books are slightly different, so here are a few notes on how this book is set out.
- Ingredients are listed in the order you use them.
- American names are given in brackets.
- We have minimised weighing to keep it simple. If you use a mug, use the American cup measure. This is equal to 250 ml/8 fl oz. Measure this into your mug to familiarise yourself with the correct level.
- Spoon measurements are level: 1 tsp = 15 ml; 1 tbsp = 15 ml.
- Eggs are medium.
- Always wash, peel, core and seed, if necessary, fresh foods before use.
- Taste and adjust seasoning to suit your own taste.
- Use butter or a margarine or spread you like, but just check the packet as some margarines or spreads are not suitable for cooking.
- Use your own discretion in substituting ingredients and personalising the recipes.
- All ovens vary, so cooking times are approximate. Always check before the recommended time is up or adjust to suit your oven.

weekly menus

Here are four weeks' menus which give you a ready-made selection of meals to make up a good, balanced diet. We've included your checklist of what you need in the cupboard or on your shopping list. Healthy eating is not faddy and it's not rocket science. This is a quick outline of what your healthy diet should contain.
- Plenty of fruit and vegetables, for vitamins, minerals, fibre – five a day is the minimum.
- A moderate amount of carbohydrates, like bread and potatoes, to fill you up and give you energy.
- A moderate amount of protein, like meat, fish and

pulses, to grow and repair your body.
- Not too much fat, like fried foods and crisps, or you'll get fat and could damage your heart.
- Not too much sugar, like cakes and puddings, for similar reasons – plus it's bad for your teeth.

week 1

meals

Monday Cottage pie (page 54)
Tuesday Turkey satay sticks (page 104)
Wednesday Filo-topped vegetable pie (page 128)
Thursday Sausage cassoulet (page 42)
Friday Tasty tuna fishcakes (page 110)
Saturday Lamb rogan josh (page 78)
Sunday Simple Sunday roast (page 90)

what you need

Cans: Borlotti or cannellini beans (1 small), sweetcorn (1 small), chopped tomatoes (1 small), tuna fish (1 small).
Dry goods and miscellaneous: Cornflour (cornstarch), egg noodles (125 g/5 oz), plain (all-purpose) flour, lager (⅔ mug), naan bread, oil, fine polenta, sugar, preferably soft brown.
Freezer: Filo pastry (4 sheets), frozen mixed vegetables, peas.
Fridge: Butter or margarine, Cheddar cheese (about 100 g/4 oz), cucumber raita, egg (1), mayonnaise, milk.
Fruit and veg: Carrots (3), courgette (1), French beans (about 100 g/4 oz), onions (4), red onion (1), new potatoes (225 g/8 oz), potatoes (8).
Meat and fish: Chicken leg portions (2), lean minced beef (225 g/8 oz), casserole lamb (350 g/12 oz), sausages (4), turkey breast steaks (2).
Spices and condiments: Chilli powder or dried chilli flakes, rogan josh curry paste, garlic purée (paste), dried mixed herbs, lemon juice, peanut butter, pesto, soy sauce, beef and vegetable stock, tomato ketchup (catsup), wine vinegar.

week 2

meals

Monday Beef and mushroom noodles (page 62)
Tuesday Creamy chicken korma (page 96)
Wednesday Minestrone (page 30)
Thursday Stir-fry turkey with noodles (page 102)
Friday Citrus salmon with stir-fried vegetables (page 112)
Saturday Spaghetti bolognese (page 58)
Sunday Sticky spare ribs (page 80)

what you need

Cans: Cannellini beans (1 small), chopped tomatoes (1 large)

Dry goods and miscellaneous: Cornflour (cornstarch), honey, dried flat rice noodles (175 g/6 oz), oil, popadoms, prawn crackers, basmati rice, spaghetti (about 175 g/6 oz), straight-to-wok noodles (300 g/ 12 oz), sugar.

Freezer: Oven chips, peas.

Fridge: Parmesan cheese, orange juice, thick plain yoghurt (150 ml/½ mug).

Fruit and veg: Broccoli (about 100 g/4 oz), carrots (2), celery stick (1), mushrooms (about 150 g/6 oz), onions (3), mixed stir-fry vegetables (350 g/12 oz pack), potato (1), red (bell) pepper (1 small), spring onions (4), stir-fried vegetables (300 g/11 oz packet).

Meat and fish: Smoked streaky bacon (2 rashers (slices)), lean minced beef (225 g/8 oz), rump steak (225 g/8 oz), skinless, boneless chicken breasts (2), pork spare ribs (700 g/1½ lb), skinned salmon steaks (2), turkey strips (225 g/8 oz).

Spices and condiments: Dried chilli flakes, korma curry paste, garlic purée (paste), bottled grated ginger, ginger purée (paste), dried mixed herbs, lemon juice, French mustard, pesto sauce, soy sauce, chicken, beef and vegetable stock, tomato ketchup (catsup), tomato purée (paste), red or white wine vinegar, red wine.

week 3

meals

Monday Cajun chicken and oven-cooked rice (page 92)
Tuesday Prawn and cashew stir-fry (page 118)
Wednesday Spicy vegetable and pasta bake (page 124)
Thursday Lamb kofte kebabs (page 56)
Friday Thai green chicken curry (page 94)
Saturday Pan-fried turkey escalopes (page 106)
Sunday Steak and mushroom pie (page 68)

what you need

Cans: Sliced bamboo shoots (1 small), coconut milk (1 large), red kidney beans (1 small), mushy peas (1 small), condensed cream of tomato soup (1 small).

Dry goods and miscellaneous: Fine breadcrumbs, plain (all-purpose) flour, unsalted cashew nuts (100 g/4 oz), honey, quick-cook noodles, oil, dried pasta, pitta breads, long grain rice.

Freezer: Oven chips, peas, sliced mixed peppers.

Fridge: Unsalted butter, Cheddar cheese (about 100 g/ 4 oz), egg, orange juice, ready-rolled puff pastry (375 g/ 13 oz packet), Greek-style yoghurt.

Fruit and veg: Coriander or mint, courgettes (zucchini) (2), lettuce, mushrooms (about 100 g/4 oz), onions (3), red (bell) pepper (½), new potatoes, sugar snap peas or mangetout (about 100 g/4 oz, baby sweetcorn (125 g/ 5 oz).

Meat and fish: Braising steak (225 g/8 oz), mini chicken fillets (450 g/1 lb), minced lamb ((225 g/8 oz), cooked, peeled prawns (100 g/4 oz), turkey escalopes (2).

Spices and condiments: Cajun seasoning, ground chilli, chilli sauce, Thai green curry paste, garlic purée (paste), ginger purée (paste), dried mixed herbs, soy sauce, beef stock, red wine, Worcestershire sauce.

week 4

meals

Monday Potato and pea frittata (page 130)
Tuesday Broccoli and cauliflower cheese (page 48)
Wednesday Pasta carbonara (page 46)
Thursday Creamy chicken and corn chowder (page 36)
Friday Chilli con carne (page 52)
Saturday Seafood paella (page 116)
Sunday Oven-roast pork with honey and mustard (page 84)

what you need

Cans: Red kidney beans (1 small), sweetcorn (1 small), chopped tomatoes (2 small).

Dry goods and miscellaneous: Bread rolls, plain (all-purpose) flour, oil, long-grain rice, pasta quills or shells, tagliatelle, sugar, preferably dark brown.

Freezer: Peas, sliced peppers, ready-to-roast potatoes and carrots, mixed cooked seafood (200 g/7 oz packet).

Fridge: Butter or margarine, Cheddar and Parmesan cheese, cream, eggs (6), milk.

Fruit and veg: Cauliflower and broccoli florets (300 g/10 oz packet), onions (4), potatoes (4), red (bell) pepper, mixed baby salad leaves, tomatoes (4).

Meat and fish: Smoked back (4 rashers (slices)) and streaky bacon (3 rashers (slices)), minced beef (225 g/8 oz), chicken (about 225 g/8 oz), pork tenderloin (1, about 250 g/9 oz).

Spices and condiments: Mild chilli powder, garlic purée (paste), dried mixed herbs, honey, Dijon and wholegrain mustard, beef, chicken and vegetable stock, tomato purée (paste), ground turmeric.

cooking the basics

You don't need full recipes for the basic things you'll cook regularly. Here's the instructions you need to cook most ordinary things.

pasta

- Bring a large pan of water to the boil. Add a pinch of salt if you want.
- Add the pasta – 2 good handfuls of small pasta shapes or 3 for large pasta shapes per person. For spaghetti, about 2.5 cm/1 in diameter bundle feeds two – feed it into the water as it softens.
- Bring back to the boil, stir, then boil gently for about 8 minutes.
- Lift out a piece with a fork and taste it carefully – it should be just soft – al dente.
- Drain well.

rice

- Bring a large pan of water to the boil. Add a pinch of salt if you want.
- Add the rice – 2 good handfuls per person.
- Bring back to the boil, stir, then boil gently for about 8 minutes.
- Meanwhile, fill and boil the kettle.
- Lift out some rice with a fork and taste it carefully – it should be just soft but not soggy.
- Drain well in a colander in the sink, then pour over the boiling water and separate the grains with a fork.

Tip: All ovens vary, so cooking times are always approximate. If you have a really old oven, expect to turn it up a bit or leave things a bit longer.

boiled root vegetables

- Wash and trim the veg. Peel only if the skin is thick and/or you don't want it (or you are going to make mash).
- Cut into similar-sized pieces, put in a pan and just cover with cold water. Add a pinch of salt if you like.
- Cover, bring to the boil, then turn down the heat so the water is simmering – bubbling gently – and cook until a sharp knife slides easily into the centre. They'll take about this long:
    whole potatoes or large vegetables: 20 minutes
    smaller potatoes or parsnips: 15 minutes
    sliced carrots: 8 minutes.
- Drain.

mashed potatoes

- Return the cooked and drained potatoes to the pan and add a knob of butter or margarine and a splash of milk.
- It's easiest to mash using a potato masher but a fork will do. Add a little more butter or margarine if necessary.

sautéed root vegetables

- Start as though boiling but only boil for half the cooking time.
- Drain well and shake in the colander to roughen the edges.
- Heat 45 ml/3 tbsp of oil in a pan, add the vegetables and fry, stirring occasionally, for about 10 minutes until golden.

Tip: Wash and trim vegetables before you start. Only peel them if you need to – old carrots, for example.

perfect roast potatoes

- I'm assuming you have a chicken or something in the oven at about 200°C/400°F/gas 6.
- Start as though boiling but only boil for half the cooking time.
- Drain well and shake in the colander to roughen the edges.
- Place around the meat and coat in the juices, or place in a baking tray with a little oil or fat.
- Cook for about 40 minutes–1 hour until crisp.

boiled green vegetables

- Wash and trim the veg and cut into similar-sized pieces.
- Bring a large pan of water to the boil. Add a pinch of salt if you want.
- Add the vegetables, bring back to the boil, then simmer until just tender. They'll take about this long:
  broccoli or cauliflower florets: 5–10 minutes
  brussels: 5 minutes
  cabbage: 4–5 minutes
  frozen veg: 2–3 minutes
  green beans: 5 minutes
  mangetout or sugar snap peas: 1–2 minutes
  peas: 4 minutes.
- Drain well.
- Spinach is different. Wash well, then put in a pan with just the water that clings to the leaves. Cook over a low heat for 2 minutes until it wilts.

steamed green vegetables

- Great for any green veg.
- If you have a steamer, just sit it on top of another pan so the steam cooks the vegetables and cook for about a minute longer than the boiling times.

microwaved green vegetables

- Place in a suitable container with just a little water.
- Cook for about a minute less than the boiling times.

roasted vegetables

- Great for a mix of potatoes, onions, aubergine, peppers, courgettes (zucchini), mushrooms and whole garlic cloves.
- Turn on the oven to 200°C/400°F/gas 6.
- Cut into even-sized chunks and put everything except the peppers, mushrooms and garlic in a baking tray.
- Sprinkle generously with olive oil and salt and stir to coat.
- Roast for 30 minutes.
- Add the remaining vegetables, stir well, then cook for a further 30 minutes.

Tip: Seasoning and spices are a matter of taste – add just how much you like.

boiled (hard-cooked) eggs

- Place in a small saucepan and just cover with cold water.
- Cover with a lid and bring to the boil.
- Cook for 3½–4 minutes for runny yolks and firm whites, 5–7 minutes for hard-boiled.

fried eggs

- Heat a teaspoon of oil in a frying pan.
- Break in the eggs and fry for about 4 minutes, spooning a little oil over the eggs as they fry.
- Remove with a fish slice as soon as they are cooked how you like them.

scrambled eggs

- Heat knob of butter or margarine in a saucepan.
- Whisk the eggs in a bowl or cup with a little salt and pepper.
- Add them to the pan and cook over a low heat, stirring all the time until the mixture scrambles but is still creamy. Do not boil.

poached eggs

- Bring a pan of water with a pinch of salt to the boil.
- Break the egg into a cup.
- Carefully pour the egg into the water, stirring round it with a spoon so the white sets rather than spreading in ribbons.
- Cook for about 3 minutes, then lift out carefully with a draining spoon.

using cook-in sauces and soups

Cook-in sauces are an easy way to add variety to your meals. Gently brown an onion and some meat in a pan, then stir in the sauce, bring to a simmer, cover and either simmer or pop in an oven at about 180°C/350°F/gas 4 until cooked through. A can of condensed soup makes an alternative sauce.

They are great for all kinds of basic ingredients.
- Chicken pieces, thighs or chunks.
- Mince of any kind.
- Stewing steak (but give it a long cooking time of at least 1½ hours).
- Lean pork pieces.
- Lamb chops or cutlets.
- Quorn.

not just beans on toast

The old favourite, beans on toast, is sometimes just what you fancy but here's a few ways to ring the changes.

- Spice up the beans with a dash of Worcestershire sauce.
- Sprinkle with grated cheese and brown under a hot grill (broiler).
- Pop a slice of ham under the beans – with or without cheese on top.
- Chop up a cooked sausage or rasher of bacon and heat up with the beans.

Tip: If you have any useful gadgets in your kitchen – mixer, blender, whatever – use them to speed things up.

not just cheese on toast

Don't just sprinkle your grated or sliced cheese on the bread and grill (broil) it, try some of these ideas.

- Spread the toast with tomato purée or ketchup, then add the cheese.
- Try a mixture of cheeses.
- If you like blue cheese, you'll love it toasted.
- Add a generous dash of Worcestershire sauce.

Tip: Change recipes as much as you like. If it works and it tastes good – it is good!

soup meals

You can throw together a delicious home-made soup so quickly and easily – and usually at a fraction of the price of ready-made versions. Have a go – you can vary the ingredients as you like – just use the recipes as a guide. If you don't have something and you don't think it will matter, it won't.

Soups are great served on their own or with crusty bread, pittas or breadsticks. Do try to use a good-quality stock or stock cube, as some are very salty and could over-season your finished soup.

minestrone

This means 'big soup' – a hearty soup that you can vary depending on the ingredients available.

SERVES 2
READY IN **30 MINUTES**

ingredients	quantity and preparation
smoked streaky bacon	2 rashers (slices)
onion	1, chopped
oil	15 ml/1 tbsp
garlic purée (paste)	5 ml/1 tsp
celery stick	1, sliced
potato	1, diced
carrot	1, diced
tomato purée (paste)	15 ml/1 tbsp
vegetable stock	600 ml/1 pt/2½ cups
salt and freshly ground black pepper	
can cannellini beans	1 small, drained and rinsed
pesto sauce	15 ml/1 tbsp
grated Parmesan cheese	15 ml/1 tbsp

1 Cut the rind off the bacon, then snip it into pieces.

2 Fry the bacon and onion in the oil for 5 minutes, stirring until soft.

3 Add the garlic, celery, potato and carrot and cook for 2 minutes, stirring.

4 Add the tomato purée, stock, salt and pepper and bring to the boil.

5 Stir in the beans and cook for 10 minutes or until the vegetables are tender.

6 Stir in the pesto and serve sprinkled with Parmesan.

main meal mulligatawny

An Anglo-Indian dish, this delicious soup is curry-flavoured with a hint of sweetness.

SERVES 2
READY IN **30 MINUTES**

ingredients	quantity and preparation
onion	1, chopped
oil	10 ml/2 tsp
mild curry paste	10–15 ml/2–3 tsp
carrot	1, diced
celery stick	1, sliced
eating (dessert) apple	1, peeled and chopped
chicken breasts	2, cut into pieces
chicken or vegetable stock	250 ml/8 fl oz/1 cup
can of chopped tomatoes	1 large
long-grain rice	50 g/2 oz/¼ cup
salt and freshly ground black pepper	
thick plain yoghurt	30 ml/2 tbsp
warm naan bread	to serve

1 Fry the onion in the oil for 5 minutes, stirring now and then until soft.

2 Stir in curry paste until well mixed. Add the carrot, celery, apple, chicken, stock and tomatoes. Bring to the boil, then half-cover and simmer for 5 minutes.

3 Sprinkle in the rice, stir, then half-cover and cook for 10–12 minutes until the rice is tender and the chicken and vegetables are cooked.

4 Add salt and pepper and swirl in the yoghurt.

5 Serve with warm naan breads.

french onion soup

If you prefer, skip step 1 and use a can of fried onions instead of fresh onions – a brilliant time-saver.

 SERVES 2
READY IN **30 MINUTES**

ingredients	quantity and preparation
butter or margarine	30 ml/2 tbsp
onions	2, sliced
garlic purée (paste)	2.5 ml/½ tsp
can of beef consommé	1 large
or beef stock	175 ml/6 fl oz/¾ cup
dry white wine	
or cider	120 ml/4 fl oz/½ cup
bay leaf	1
French stick	1 small, sliced
Gruyère or Cheddar	
cheese	about 50 g/2 oz, grated
salt and freshly	
ground black pepper	

1 Melt the butter or margarine and fry the onions for at least 10 minutes until very soft and golden brown, stirring now and then.

2 Stir in the garlic, then add the consommé or stock, wine or cider, and bay leaf. Half-cover the pan with a lid and simmer for 10 minutes.

3 Lightly toast the French bread slices on both sides. Sprinkle one side thickly with the cheese and grill (broil) until golden brown.

4 Discard the bay leaf. Taste the soup and season with salt and pepper if needed. Serve with a piece of toasted cheese floating on the top of each bowl, with extras served separately.

creamy chicken and corn chowder

Try this with turkey, smoked mackerel, canned salmon or cooked prawns instead of chicken.

SERVES 2
READY IN **15 MINUTES**

ingredients	quantity and preparation
butter or margarine	15 ml/1 tbsp
onion	1, chopped
plain (all-purpose) flour	15 ml/1 tbsp
chicken stock	300 ml/½ pt/1¼ cups
dried mixed herbs	a pinch
cooked chicken	225 g/8 oz/1 cup, diced
can of sweetcorn	1 small
salt and freshly ground black pepper	
milk	150 ml/¼ pt/⅔ cup
warm buttered bread rolls	to serve

1 Heat the butter or margarine and fry the onion for 5 minutes, stirring now and then until soft.

2 Sprinkle the flour over the onion and cook for a few seconds, stirring. Gradually add the stock, stirring. Add the herbs and bring to the boil.

3 Add the chicken, sweetcorn, salt and pepper. Simmer, without a lid, for 5 minutes.

4 Stir in the milk and heat until steaming hot but not boiling.

5 Serve straight away with warm buttered rolls.

quick vegetable soup

Try your favourite vegetables in whatever combination you prefer, or use frozen mixed vegetables.

 SERVES 2
READY IN **25 MINUTES**

ingredients	quantity and preparation
onion	1, finely chopped
oil	15 ml/1 tbsp
chopped mixed vegetables, such as carrots, celery cabbage, courgettes (zucchini), potatoes	450 g/1 lb/3 cups
vegetable stock	450 ml/¾ pt/2 cups
bay leaf	1
dried mixed herbs	5 ml/1 tsp
milk or single (light) cream	45 ml/3 tbsp
salt and freshly ground black pepper	
wholemeal toast or crusty bread rolls	to serve

1 Fry the onion in the oil for 5 minutes, stirring now and then until soft.

2 Stir in the vegetables and cook for 3 minutes.

3 Add the stock, bay leaf and herbs. Cover and simmer for 10 minutes until the vegetables are tender.

4 Turn off the heat and stir in the milk or cream. Remove the bay leaf and season to taste with salt and pepper.

5 For a chunky soup, blend half the soup in a food processor. For a completely smooth soup, purée all the mixture.

6 Serve with hot buttered toast or crusty rolls.

traditional chicken noodle soup

Guaranteed to remind you of home, use chilled stock or a good-quality stock cube.

SERVES 2
READY IN **15 MINUTES**

ingredients	quantity and preparation
chicken stock	300 ml/½ pt/1¼ cups
soup noodles or pasta	50 g/2 oz
can of condensed cream of chicken soup	300 g/11 oz/1 med
soured cream	30 ml/2 tbsp
chopped fresh parsley	10 ml/2 tsp

1 Bring the stock to the boil in a pan, add the noodles or pasta and cook according to the packet instructions.

2 Add the soup and heat through. Stir in the soured cream. Sprinkle with the parsley.

3 Serve with fresh bread.

sausage and bacon favourites

Sausages and bacon are two great stand-bys, but they are more versatile than you might think. Stretch your imagination a little and with just a few extra ingredients they can be transformed into brilliant brunches and super-quick suppers.

Treat yourself to a decent non-stick frying pan and you'll find that both sausages and bacon can be dry-fried without extra fat because they have enough of their own. After cooking, to dispose of the fat, let it cool in the pan, then wipe away with kitchen paper. Never pour it down the sink.

sausage cassoulet

A quick and easy version of a classic dish, you can use any kind of beans in any combination for this.

 SERVES 2
READY IN **30 MINUTES**

ingredients	quantity and preparation
sausages	4
onion	1, chopped
garlic purée (paste)	5 ml/1 tsp
plain (all-purpose) flour	5 ml/1 tsp
beef or vegetable stock or a mixture of stock, wine or cider	250 ml/8 fl oz/1 cup
can of borlotti or cannellini beans	1 small, drained and rinsed
can of chopped tomatoes	1 small
dried mixed herbs	2.5 ml/½ tsp
salt and freshly ground black pepper	
mashed potatoes and French beans	to serve

1 Dry-fry the sausages until lightly browned all over. Remove from the pan and cut into bite-sized pieces.

2 Drain off most of the fat, leaving about 10 ml/ 2 tsp in the pan. Fry the onion for 5 minutes. Stir in the garlic, then sprinkle over the flour and stir in.

3 Stir in the stock, a little at a time. Return the sausage pieces to the pan with the beans, tomatoes and herbs. Season to taste with salt and pepper.

4 Half-cover and simmer for 15 minutes or until the onions are tender and the sausage cooked.

5 Serve with mashed potatoes and a green vegetable such as French beans.

spicy sausage pasta

A satisfying and well-balanced meal. A chunky pasta is best, but you can use whatever you have.

SERVES 2
READY IN **20 MINUTES**

ingredients	quantity and preparation
penne pasta	225 g/8 oz/ 2 cups
spicy sausages, pork, beef or vegetarian	6
onion	1, chopped
garlic purée (paste)	5 ml/1 tsp
can of chopped tomatoes	1 large
dried mixed herbs	2.5 ml/½ tsp
salt and freshly ground black pepper	
grated Cheddar cheese (optional)	to serve

1 Cook the pasta in a pan of boiling water for 10 minutes or according to the packet instructions, until tender. Drain, then tip back into the pan and cover to keep the pasta hot. If it needs to stand for a few minutes, leave a very little water in the pan to prevent the pasta from sticking.

2 Dry-fry the sausages, turning often, until well browned and cooked through. Cut them into bite-sized pieces.

3 Drain most of the fat and juices from the pan, leaving about 10 ml/2 tsp behind, then fry the onion for 5 minutes until softened and beginning to brown.

4 Stir in the garlic. Add the tomatoes, herbs, salt and pepper. Cook uncovered for 5 minutes.

5 Add the sausages and drained pasta to the pan. Cook for 1 minute or until everything is heated through. Serve sprinkled with grated cheese, if you like.

pasta carbonara

Italian-style eggs and bacon, this classic recipe is quick and easy – it's also good with spaghetti.

SERVES 2
READY IN **20 MINUTES**

ingredients	quantity and preparation
tagliatelle or pasta quills or shells	175 g/6 oz/1½ cups
streaky bacon	3 rashers (slices), rinded
eggs	2
cream or milk	30 ml/2 tbsp
Parmesan cheese	25 g/1 oz, grated
salt and freshly ground black pepper	
garlic purée (paste)	5 ml/1 tsp
mixed baby salad leaves	to serve

1 Cook the pasta in a pan of boiling salted water for 10 minutes or according to the packet instructions, until tender.

2 While the pasta is cooking, cut the rind off the bacon, then snip the bacon into small pieces.

3 Break the eggs into a bowl, then add the cream or milk, about half of the cheese, and some salt and pepper. Whisk together with a fork.

4 About 5 minutes before the pasta is ready, dry-fry the bacon until lightly browned and crispy. Stir in the garlic and cook for a few more seconds.

5 Drain the pasta and return it to the hot pan. Add the bacon and the egg mixture and stir gently for 1 minute, until the pasta is coated and there is no liquid egg mixture left.

6 Sprinkle the rest of the cheese over the carbonara and serve with mixed baby salad leaves.

broccoli and cauliflower cheese

You can sprinkle the finished dish with extra cheese and brown in a hot oven if you like.

SERVES 2
READY IN **25 MINUTES**

ingredients	quantity and preparation
cauliflower and broccoli florets	300 g/10 oz packet
smoked back bacon	4 rashers (slices)
butter or margarine	30 ml/2 tbsp
plain (all-purpose) flour	30 ml/2 tbsp
Dijon mustard	2.5 ml/½ tsp
milk	300 ml/½ pt/1¼ cups
Cheddar cheese	75 g/3 oz, grated
salt and freshly ground black pepper	
sliced tomato salad	to serve

1 Cook the cauliflower in boiling lightly salted water for 4 minutes. Add the broccoli and cook for a further 4 minutes or until both are just tender but not soft. Drain well.

2 Meanwhile, cut the rind off the bacon, then snip the bacon into small pieces.

3 Dry-fry the bacon for 4 minutes until browned and crispy.

4 Melt the butter or margarine in a saucepan and stir in the flour and mustard. Pour in a little of the milk and stir together until smooth and thick. Stir in the rest of the milk. Bring to the boil, stirring with a wooden spoon or whisk, until thickened. Simmer for 2 minutes, then turn off the heat.

5 Stir in the cheese and season with salt and pepper.

6 Pour the cheese sauce over the broccoli and cauliflower and scatter with the bacon. Serve with a sliced tomato salad.

toad in the hole

For a change, try this with chops instead of sausages, or use some spiced or herby sausages.

SERVES 2
READY IN **45 MINUTES**

ingredients	quantity and preparation
pork sausages	6
oil	15 ml/1 tbsp
egg	1
milk	150 ml/¼ pt/⅔ cup
plain (all-purpose) flour	50 g/2 oz/½ cup
salt	a pinch
baked beans or peas	to serve

1 Turn on the oven to 220°C/425°F/gas 7. Prick the sausages and place with the oil in a small roasting tin in the oven for 10 minutes.

2 Whisk the egg and milk into the flour and salt in a bowl until smooth. Pour over the sausages, return to the oven, then turn the temperature down to 200°C/400°F/gas 6.

3 Cook for 25 minutes until risen and golden brown. Serve with baked beans or peas.

mince

Mince is so undervalued. It is versatile and inexpensive – plus it forms the basis of many of our comfort-food favourites. It features in all kinds of familiar dishes: Italian spaghetti bolognese, Mexican chilli con carne and American burgers. Plus, we've included favourites like cottage pie, spicy lamb kofte kebabs and beef curry.

If money is really tight, you can stretch mince even further by adding inexpensive ingredients like pasta, tomatoes and baked beans. Most types of mince can be swapped for other kinds in the recipes. Vegetarians can use minced Quorn or soya, except for burgers and meatballs.

chilli con carne

A great way to make mince as spicy as you like, make it go further by using a large can of beans.

SERVES 2
READY IN **50 MINUTES**

ingredients	quantity and preparation
onion	1, chopped
garlic purée (paste)	5 ml/1 tsp
oil	15 ml/1 tbsp
lean minced beef	225 g/8 oz
mild chilli powder	5 ml/1 tsp
beef stock	250 ml/8 fl oz/1 cup
can of red kidney beans	1 small, drained and rinsed
can of chopped tomatoes	1 small
tomato purée (paste)	10 ml/2 tsp
sugar, preferably dark brown	2.5 ml/½ tsp
dried mixed herbs	2.5 ml/½ tsp
salt and pepper	
boiled rice	to serve

1 Fry the onion and garlic in the oil over a moderate heat for 5 minutes.

2 Stir in the beef and cook for 5 minutes until it is well browned. Break up the lumps of meat with a wooden spoon as it cooks.

3 Stir in the chilli powder, then add the stock, kidney beans, tomatoes, tomato purée, sugar, herbs, salt and pepper.

4 Bring to the boil, then simmer, half-covered, for 30 minutes.

5 Serve with boiled rice.

cottage pie

Try this with lamb mince, in which case it's shepherd's pie, or why not try it with turkey mince?

SERVES 2
READY IN **55 MINUTES**

ingredients	quantity and preparation
potatoes	4, cut into chunks
butter or margarine	30 ml/2 tbsp
milk	30 ml/2 tbsp
salt and freshly ground black pepper	
onion	1, chopped
oil	15 ml/1 tbsp
lean minced beef	225 g/8 oz
beef stock	120 ml/4 fl oz/½ cup
carrot	1, diced
dried mixed herbs	2.5 ml/½ tsp
tomato ketchup (catsup)	15 ml/1 tbsp
soy sauce	5 ml/1 tsp
frozen peas	1 handful

1 Cook the potatoes in boiling water for 15 minutes until tender. Drain well and mash with the butter or margarine, milk, salt and pepper.

2 Fry the onion in the oil for 5 minutes.

3 Add the minced beef. Turn up the heat a little and cook for 5 minutes, stirring and breaking up the meat with a wooden spoon, until browned.

4 Add the stock, carrot, herbs, ketchup and soy sauce. Season with salt and pepper.

5 Bring to the boil, then simmer, uncovered, for 20 minutes until well-reduced. Turn off the heat and stir in the peas.

6 Turn on the oven to 200°C/400°F/gas 6. Spoon the meat mixture into an ovenproof dish. Top with mashed potato and bake for 25 minutes.

lamb kofte kebabs

So much tastier than takeaway, and much cheaper. You'll find ginger purée on the spice shelves.

SERVES 2
READY IN **30 MINUTES**

ingredients	quantity and preparation
minced lamb	225 g/8 oz
garlic purée (paste)	5 ml/1 tsp
ginger purée (paste)	5 ml/1 tsp
ground chilli	2.5 ml/½ tsp
salt and freshly ground black pepper	
oil	10 ml/2 tsp
pitta breads	2
Greek-style yoghurt	60 ml/4 tbsp
fresh or frozen chopped coriander or mint	15 ml/1 tbsp
shredded lettuce	

1 Put the lamb, garlic, ginger, chilli, salt and pepper in a bowl. Mix together using your hands. Shape into 10 small balls.

2 Fry the meatballs in the oil over a moderate heat for 10 minutes, turning often until well browned and cooked through. Drain on kitchen paper.

3 Warm the pitta breads under the grill (broiler) or in the microwave for a few seconds. Cut each in half and open up to make a pocket.

4 Mix together the yoghurt with the coriander or mint and salt and pepper. Fill the pitta pockets with shredded lettuce, meatballs and yoghurt mixture.

spaghetti bolognese

While you are cooking, make double
the quantity and freeze half or turn
half into lasagne for another day.

SERVES 2
READY IN **40 MINUTES**

ingredients	quantity and preparation
onion	1, chopped
carrot	1 small, chopped
red (bell) pepper	1 small, chopped
garlic purée (paste)	5 ml/1 tsp
oil	15 ml/1 tbsp
lean minced beef	225 g/8 oz
mushrooms	50 g/2 oz
can of chopped tomatoes	1 large
beef stock or red wine	75 ml/5 tbsp
tomato purée (paste)	15 ml/1 tbsp
dried mixed herbs	5 ml/1 tsp
salt and freshly ground black pepper	
spaghetti	175 g/6 oz
Parmesan cheese	50 g/2 oz, grated

1 Fry the onion, carrot, pepper and garlic in the oil for 5 minutes.

2 Add the minced beef. Turn up the heat a little and cook for 5 minutes, stirring and breaking up the meat with a wooden spoon, until browned.

3 Add the mushrooms, tomatoes, stock or wine, tomato purée and herbs. Season with salt and pepper.

4 Bring to the boil, then simmer, half-covered, for 20 minutes.

5 Meanwhile, cook the spaghetti in plenty of boiling salted water according to packet instructions. Drain.

6 Pile the spaghetti on to plates, top with the meat sauce and sprinkle the cheese on top.

beef and pepper linguine

If you think this looks too simple to be really tasty, give it the benefit of the doubt and try it.

SERVES 2
READY IN **30 MINUTES**

ingredients	quantity and preparation
linguine	175 g/6 oz
salt and pepper	
minced (ground) beef	225 g/8 oz
onion	1, chopped
green (bell) pepper	1, diced
garlic purée	2.5 ml/½ tsp
soy sauce	30 ml/2 tbsp

1 Cook the linguine in a pan of boiling salted water for about 8 minutes until just tender, then drain. Meanwhile fry the beef, onion, pepper and garlic purée in a large pan for about 5 minutes until the meat is no longer pink. Drain off any excess fat.

2 Remove from the heat and gently stir in the linguine and soy sauce. Season to taste with salt and pepper and serve.

beef

The trick to tender beef on the plate is choosing the right cut. For quick-cook dishes, you need a lean, tender cut – more expensive but there's little waste and a little will go a long way. For slow-cooked dishes, choose a cheaper cut labelled for braising or casseroling. If in doubt, ask your butcher or at the supermarket meat counter.

You can make any meat go further by adding starchy carbohydrates such as potatoes, pasta and rice. Store meat in the coldest part of the fridge and, if raw, keep it away from cooked foods. Be guided by the 'use-by' date, but most joints, chops and steaks will keep in the fridge for 2–3 days.

beef and mushroom noodles

This is great to make when steak is on special offer – or you can use strips of chicken instead.

SERVES 2
READY IN **20 MINUTES**

ingredients	quantity and preparation
rump steak	350 g/12 oz
cornflour (cornstarch)	5 ml/1 tsp
salt and freshly ground black pepper	
oil	20 ml/4 tsp
broccoli florets	about 100 g/4 oz, cut into small pieces
beef stock or water	60 ml/4 tbsp
mushrooms	50 g/2 oz, sliced
spring onions (scallions)	4, sliced
soy sauce	15 ml/1 tbsp
straight-to-wok medium or thick noodles	300 g/12 oz
prawn crackers	to serve

1 Slice the beef into long strips. Mix together the cornflour, salt and pepper and toss the beef in this mixture until lightly coated.

2 Fry the beef in a frying pan in half the oil over a high heat for 1 minute, stirring until browned. Remove from the pan.

3 Add the rest of the oil, the broccoli and stock or water. Cover and cook for 3 minutes.

4 Add the mushrooms and spring onions and stir-fry for 2 minutes.

5 Stir in the soy sauce, noodles and beef. Cook for 2 minutes, stirring until hot.

6 Serve with prawn crackers.

beef in beer

Great for celebrations, this takes a while to cook, but needs no attention once it's in the oven.

SERVES 2
READY IN **90 MINUTES**

ingredients	quantity and preparation
braising steak	350 g/12 oz, cubed
oil	15–30 ml/1–2 tbsp
onion	1, sliced
garlic purée (paste)	5 ml/1 tsp
sugar, preferably brown	5 ml/1 tsp
plain (all-purpose) flour	15 ml/1 tbsp
light ale or beer	120 ml/4 fl oz/½ cup
beef stock	120 ml/4 fl oz/½ cup
dried mixed herbs	2.5 ml/½ tsp
salt and freshly ground black pepper	
Creamy mash or jacket potatoes and carrots or a green vegetable to serve	

1 Fry the beef in half the oil over a high heat for 3 minutes, turning until well browned. Lift out on to a plate.

2 Add the rest of the oil and the onion to the pan and fry over a medium heat for 5 minutes.

3 Stir in the garlic and sugar. Sprinkle over the flour and stir in. Gradually add the beer, stirring until thickened.

4 Return the beef to the pan with the stock, herbs, salt and pepper.

5 Bring to the boil, then turn down the heat, half-cover and gently simmer for 1 hour.

6 Serve with creamy mash or jacket potatoes with carrots or a green vegetable.

beef goulash

This classic Hungarian dish takes a little time, but you can relax while it cooks itself.

 SERVES 2
READY IN **120 MINUTES**

ingredients	quantity and preparation
plain (all-purpose) flour	10 ml/2 tsp
salt and freshly ground black pepper	
braising steak	350 g/12 oz, cubed
onion	1, sliced
oil	15 ml/1 tbsp
garlic purée (paste)	5 ml/1 tsp
ground paprika	10 ml/2 tsp
dried mixed herbs	2.5 ml/½ tsp
can of chopped tomatoes	1 small
beef stock	75 ml/5 tbsp
red (bell) pepper	1, seeded and sliced
soured cream	30 ml/2 tbsp
buttered noodles or jacket potatoes	to serve

1 Mix together the flour, salt and pepper and toss the beef in this mixture to lightly coat.

2 Fry the onion in half of the oil in an ovenproof casserole for 5 minutes.

3 Add the garlic and cook for 1 minute. Transfer to a plate.

4 Fry the beef in the rest of the oil, turning until browned on all sides.

5 Sprinkle over the paprika and herbs and stir. Return the onion and garlic to the casserole with the tomatoes, stock and pepper slices. Stir and bring to the boil.

6 Turn on the oven to 160°C/325°F/gas 3. Cover with a lid or foil and cook in the oven for 1½ hours or until the meat is tender.

7 Stir the beef mixture. Top with soured cream and serve with buttered noodles or jacket potatoes (cooked in the oven at the same time).

steak and mushroom pie

Sure to impress your friends, you can buy braising steak – ideal for long cooking – in slabs or ready cubed.

 SERVES 2
READY IN **90 MINUTES**

ingredients	quantity and preparation
braising steak	350 g/12 oz, cubed
oil	30 ml/2 tbsp
onion	1, chopped
mushrooms	about 50 g/2 oz, sliced
plain (all-purpose) flour	15 ml/1 tbsp
beef stock	120 ml/4 fl oz/½ cup
red wine or stock	60 ml/4 tbsp
Worcestershire sauce	5 ml/1 tsp
dried mixed herbs	a pinch
salt and freshly ground black pepper	
ready-rolled puff pastry	375 g/13 oz packet
new potatoes or mash and peas	to serve

1 Fry the beef in half of the oil, turning until browned on all sides. Lift on to a plate.

2 Fry the onion in the rest of the oil for 5 minutes, stirring. Add the mushrooms and cook for 3 minutes.

3 Sprinkle in the flour, then gradually stir in the stock, then the wine or extra stock.

4 Return the beef to the pan with the Worcestershire sauce, herbs, salt and pepper.

5 Bring to the boil, stirring. Turn down the heat and simmer, half-covered, for 30 minutes until the beef is tender. Tip the mixture into a pie dish. Turn on the oven to 200°C/400°F/gas 6.

6 Leave the pastry at room temperature for 5 minutes, then carefully unroll. Dampen the edge of the dish with cold water. Cut off a 2.5 cm strip of pastry and put around the edge of the dish. Dampen the pastry rim with water, then put the large piece of pastry on top.

7 Press the edges together, trim and decorate with pastry shapes if you like. Brush the top with milk. Make a small slit in the top and bake for 30 minutes until well risen and brown.

8 Serve with new potatoes or mash and peas.

steak with shallots and wine

A nice Cabernet will be perfect for this – but any bottle of red will make a tasty dish.

SERVES 2
READY IN **25 MINUTES**

ingredients	quantity and preparation
beef steaks	2
oil	15 ml/1 tbsp
salt and pepper	
shallots	2, very finely chopped
butter or margarine	30 ml/2 tbsp
red wine	150 ml/¼ pt/2/3 cup

1 Fry the steaks in hot oil until brown on both sides, then cook for a further 5–10 minutes until cooked to your liking. Lift out of the pan and season with salt and pepper.

2 Add the shallot to the pan and cook in the meat juices for about 5 minutes until translucent, then add a little of the butter or margarine if the pan seems dry.

3 Add the wine, bring to the boil and simmer until reduced by a third. Take off the heat, swirl in the remaining butter and spoon over.

lamb

Lamb is quite expensive but very versatile and delicious. You can use minced lamb instead of minced beef in the mince chapters, too, to give you more options. Long, slow cooking will give you succulent, tender results with casserole lamb, whereas chops or cutlets can be cooked more quickly and left slightly pink in the centre to ensure they are moist and juicy.

moroccan lamb with couscous

This sounds exotic but is really simple to make – and absolutely delicious with a lovely sweet edge.

SERVES 2
READY IN **90 MINUTES**

ingredients	quantity and preparation
casserole lamb, cubed	350 g/12 oz
onion	1, chopped
tomato purée (paste)	15 ml/1 tbsp
garlic purée (paste)	5 ml/1 tsp
ginger purée (paste)	5 ml/1 tsp
dried chilli flakes	a pinch
ground cinnamon	a pinch
vegetable stock	375 ml/13 fl oz/1½ cups
salt and freshly ground black pepper	
courgette (zucchini)	1, diced
yellow (bell) pepper	1, diced
ready-to-eat apricots	4, chopped
For the couscous **vegetable stock**	150 ml/¼ pt/⅔ cup
couscous	100 g/4 oz/½ cup

1 Put the lamb, onion, tomato purée, garlic purée, ginger purée, chilli flakes and cinnamon in a saucepan. Add the stock and season with salt and pepper.

2 Bring to the boil, then stir, lower the heat and simmer, half-covered, for 45 minutes, stirring occasionally.

3 Stir in the courgette, yellow pepper and apricots and cook for 30 minutes or until the meat and vegetables are tender.

4 For the couscous, bring the stock to the boil in a saucepan. Add the couscous, stir, then turn off the heat. Cover with a lid and leave for 10 minutes.

5 Fluff up the couscous with a fork and serve with the lamb.

lancashire hot-pot

This is an easy version of a much-loved classic, traditionally made with lamb and potatoes.

SERVES 2
READY IN **105 MINUTES**

ingredients	quantity and preparation
onions	2, cut lengthways into 6 wedges
oil	30 ml/2 tbsp
casserole lamb	350 g/12 oz, cubed
garlic purée (paste)	5 ml/1 tsp
plain (all-purpose) flour	30 ml/2 tbsp
lamb or vegetable stock	450 ml/¾ pt/2 cups
carrots	2
potatoes	2
salt and freshly ground black pepper	
green vegetable	to serve

1 Turn on the oven to 160°C/325°F/gas 3.

2 Fry the onions in the oil in a flameproof casserole dish over a moderate heat for 3 minutes, then add the lamb and cook for 3 minutes, stirring until browned all over.

3 Stir in the garlic purée, then sprinkle over the flour and stir.

4 Add the stock a little at a time, stirring until thickened.

5 Cut the carrots and potatoes into bite-sized chunks and add to the casserole. Season with salt and pepper. Bring to the boil.

6 Stir, then cover with a lid (or foil) and cook in the oven for 1½ hours. Serve with a green vegetable such as broccoli.

oven-baked lamb biryani

You can make this with beef for a change; the slow cooking will make it meltingly tender.

SERVES 2
READY IN **75 MINUTES**

ingredients	quantity and preparation
lamb	350 g/12 oz, cubed
oil	15 ml/1 tbsp
onion	1, sliced
mushrooms	50 g/2 oz, halved
curry paste	15 ml/1 tbsp
can of chopped tomatoes	1 small
vegetable stock	250 ml/8 fl oz/1 cup
salt and freshly ground black pepper	
frozen peas	50 g/2 oz/¼ cup
basmati rice	100 g/4 oz/½ cup
water	300 ml/½ pt/1¼ cups
naan bread or chapattis	to serve

1 Fry the lamb in the oil over a medium-high heat for 3 minutes, turning often until browned all over. Lift out of the pan on to a plate.

2 Add the onion to the pan and fry gently for 7 minutes until soft and beginning to brown.

3 Stir in the mushrooms and curry paste and cook for 1 minute.

4 Add the tomatoes, stock, salt and pepper and bring to the boil. Turn down the heat, half-cover and simmer for 20 minutes.

5 Turn off the heat and stir in the peas.

6 Rinse the rice in a sieve under cold running water. Tip into a pan. Add the water and bring to the boil. Simmer for 7 minutes until it is almost cooked. Drain well.

7 Turn on the oven to 160°C/325°F/gas 3.

8 Spoon half the rice into a greased casserole dish. Spoon the lamb curry on top. Cover with the rest of the rice. Cover with a lid (or foil) and bake in the oven for 30 minutes.

9 Serve with warm naan bread or chapattis.

lamb rogan josh

Try making this recipe with a different curry paste for a change, or substitute beef or chicken.

SERVES 2
READY IN **75 MINUTES**

ingredients	quantity and preparation
casserole lamb	350 g/12 oz, cubed
onion	1, chopped
carrot, diced	1, diced
oil	15–30 ml/1–2 tbsp
rogan josh curry paste	30 ml/2 tbsp
lager	150 ml/¼ pt/⅔ cup
salt and pepper	
naan bread and cucumber raita	to serve

1 Brown the lamb, onion and carrot in the oil. Stir in the curry paste and cook for 1 minute. Pour in the lager, bring to the boil and season.

2 Reduce the heat, half-cover and simmer gently for 45 minutes or until tender.

3 Serve with naan bread and a cucumber raita.

pork

Always make sure you cook pork thoroughly and be particularly careful to store it well wrapped and not to exceed the use-by dates. As with all meats, long slow cooking tenderises the meat and may yield the best results, except for particular cuts. Pork can be stringy if not adequately cooked.

Pork goes particularly well with contrasting flavours, and the retro favourite pork and pineapple never goes out of fashion.

sticky spare ribs

Fabulous finger food – you'll need plenty of napkins and a finger bowl with this dish!

SERVES 2
READY IN **75 MINUTES**

ingredients	quantity and preparation
pork spare ribs	700 g/1½ lb
garlic purée (paste)	5 ml/1 tsp
ginger purée (paste)	5 ml/1 tsp
clear honey	30 ml/2 tbsp
tomato ketchup (catsup)	30 ml/2 tbsp
soy sauce	30 ml/2 tbsp
French mustard	5 ml/1 tsp
red or white vinegar	10 ml/2 tsp
dried chilli flakes	a pinch
salt and freshly ground black pepper	
oven chips	to serve

1 Turn on the oven to 200°C/400°F/gas 6. Put the spare ribs in a large roasting tin in a single layer.

2 Mix all the remaining ingredients together in a jug. Brush a little of the sauce all over the ribs.

3 Roast, uncovered, for 20 minutes, then turn over and roast for a further 20 minutes. Pour off any fat from the roasting tin.

4 Turn down the oven to 180°C/350°F/gas 4. Brush the ribs with the rest of the sauce.

5 Roast for another 30 minutes or until the pork is tender and the sauce thick and sticky.

6 Serve with oven chips.

gammon with pineapple relish

A sophisticated sweet and sour, gammon and pineapple – a take on the old 80s favourite.

 SERVES 2
READY IN **25 MINUTES**

ingredients	quantity and preparation
pineapple chunks in natural juice	1 small can
soft light brown sugar	10 ml/2 tsp
wine vinegar	10 ml/2 tsp
ginger purée (paste)	5 ml/1 tsp
chopped fresh or frozen parsley or coriander	15 ml/1 tbsp
or dried mixed herbs	a large pinch
gammon steaks	2
freshly ground black pepper	
boiled rice and peas	to serve

1 Roughly chop the pineapple chunks, then put in a pan with the juice, sugar, vinegar and ginger. Add the dried herbs, if using.

2 Simmer uncovered for 15 minutes or until the juice has evaporated and the relish is thick. Stir in the fresh herbs, if using.

3 Season the gammon steaks with pepper and grill (broil) for 4 minutes on each side until cooked through.

4 Serve the gammon with the relish, boiled rice and peas.

oven-roast pork with honey and mustard

This cooks to a delicious, slightly sticky and sweet glaze. Do make sure pork is well cooked.

SERVES 2
READY IN **20 MINUTES**

ingredients	quantity and preparation
garlic purée (paste)	5 ml/1 tsp
honey	15 ml/1 tbsp
wholegrain mustard	5 ml/1 tsp
oil	15 ml/1 tbsp
salt and freshly ground black pepper	
pork tenderloin	1, about 250 g/9 oz
ready-to-roast potatoes and carrots	to serve

1 Turn on the oven to 200°C/400°F/gas 6.

2 Mix together the garlic, honey, mustard, oil, salt and pepper

3 Cut the tenderloin in half widthways and brush both pieces all over with the honey mixture.

4 Place in a small roasting tin and cook in the oven for 20 minutes until well browned and the juices run clear when pierced with the tip of a knife.

5 Cut into slices and serve with roast potatoes and carrots.

herb and onion pork

If you like, you can brown the pork chops first in a little oil in a frying pan before putting in the parcel.

SERVES 2
READY IN **60 MINUTES**

ingredients	quantity and preparation
onion	1, sliced
potato	1, diced
eating apple	1, quartered, cored and sliced
frozen peas	a handful
salt and pepper	
pork chops	2
dried mixed herbs	5 ml/1 tsp

1 Turn on the oven to 190°C/375°F/gas 5.

2 Layer the onion, potato, apple and peas with salt and pepper on a 30 cm/12 in square of lightly greased foil. Top with the pork chops, then sprinkle with the herbs.

3 Twist the foil to seal, place on a baking sheet and bake for 45 minutes until cooked through.

chicken

When it comes to fast and easy cooking, chicken is hard to beat and has become a real favourite. Lean and healthy, it's full of protein and there are loads of different cuts which are great when cooking for just one or two.

Always check the use-by date and make sure the meat looks really fresh, then get it into a fridge as soon as possible, well wrapped. Wash your hands before and after handling and never use the same utensils for preparing raw poultry and cooked foods. If freezing, store for up to 3 months, and thaw completely before cooking. Always cook thoroughly and check that it is done by piercing the meat at the thickest point – the juices should run clear.

one-pot chicken

Very little washing up is always good
– plus this is an easy and tasty recipe
everyone will enjoy!

SERVES 2
READY IN **45 MINUTES**

ingredients	quantity and preparation
skinless, boneless chicken breasts	2
or skinned chicken thighs	4
oil	30 ml/2 tbsp
onion	1, chopped
garlic purée (paste)	5 ml/1 tsp
plain (all-purpose) flour	5 ml/1 tsp
can of chopped tomatoes	1 small
yellow (bell) pepper	1, sliced
potatoes	2, cubed
hot chicken stock	120 ml/4 fl oz/½ cup
dried mixed herbs	2.5 ml/½ tsp
salt and freshly ground black pepper	

1 If using chicken breasts, cut each one into 3 pieces. Fry the chicken over a high heat in 15 ml/1 tbsp of the oil for 2 minutes, turning until brown on all sides. Lift out and put on a plate.

2 Add the remaining oil and fry the onion for 5 minutes, stirring. Stir in the garlic and cook for 1 minute.

3 Sprinkle the flour over the onion and stir in, then mix in the chopped tomatoes a little at a time.

4 Add the pepper, potatoes, stock, herbs, salt and pepper. Bring to the boil, then return the chicken to the pan.

5 Cover with a lid and simmer gently for 25 minutes, or until the chicken and potatoes are cooked.

simple sunday roast

Cooking Sunday roast with all the
trimmings can be simple – as this
one-pan dish shows.

SERVES 2
READY IN **60 MINUTES**

ingredients	quantity and preparation
chicken leg portions	2
oil	10 ml/2 tsp
lemon juice	10 ml/2 tsp
dried mixed herbs	a pinch
salt and freshly ground black pepper	
For the roasted vegetables	
carrot	1
red onion	1
even-sized new potatoes	225 g/8 oz
oil	15–30 ml/1–2 tbsp
courgette (zucchini)	1

1 Gently ease up the skin from the chicken. Mix together the oil, lemon juice, herbs, salt and pepper. Rub this over the chicken flesh under the skin.

2 Turn the oven on to 200°C/400°F/gas 6 and put a roasting tin in the oven.

3 Cut the carrot into chunks. Cut the onion into 6 wedges.

4 Put the carrot, onion and potatoes in a bowl. Drizzle over 15 ml/1 tbsp of the oil and sprinkle with salt and pepper. Turn the vegetables in the oil to coat.

5 Tip the vegetables into the hot roasting tin on one side, spreading out into a single layer. Place the chicken portions on the other side of the tin. Cook in the oven for 20 minutes.

6 Cut the courgette into chunks and coat in the rest of the oil.

7 Add the courgettes to the tin, then turn all the vegetables over so that they brown evenly.

8 Roast for another 20 minutes (check half-way through and turn the vegetables if some are browning unevenly), until the chicken and vegetables are cooked through.

cajun chicken and oven-cooked rice

Add some garlic bread to the oven, too, if you have good appetite, and perhaps serve with a mixed salad.

SERVES 2
READY IN **45 MINUTES**

ingredients	quantity and preparation
onion	1, chopped
oil	30 ml/2 tbsp
long grain rice	100 g/4 oz/½ cup
hot stock or water	450 ml/¾ pt/2 cups
can of red kidney beans	1 small, drained and rinsed
salt and freshly ground black pepper	
plain (all-purpose) flour	15 ml/1 tbsp
Cajun seasoning	2.5 ml/½ tsp
mini chicken fillets	225 g/8 oz

1 Turn on the oven to 200°C/400°F/gas 6.

2 Fry the onion in 15 ml/1 tbsp of the oil for 5 minutes until soft.

3 Rinse the rice in a sieve under cold running water. Add to the onions and cook, stirring, for 1 minute.

4 Tip the onion and rice mixture into an ovenproof dish. Stir in the stock or water, kidney beans, salt and pepper.

5 Cover with a lid or foil, put on the middle shelf of the oven and cook for 15–20 minutes.

6 Meanwhile, mix together the flour, Cajun seasoning and a pinch of salt. Toss the chicken fillets in the flour mixture.

7 Brush a non-stick baking tray with the remaining oil, then spread out the chicken fillets in a single layer. Bake on the top shelf of the oven for about 15 minutes, turning over half-way through cooking time.

8 Check that the chicken is cooked by cutting a piece in half and that the rice is tender before serving.

thai green chicken curry

Try this with pork fillet or turkey. If you use creamed coconut, blend it with a little boiling water.

SERVES 2
READY IN **25 MINUTES**

ingredients	quantity and preparation
mini chicken fillets	225 g/8 oz
oil	30 ml/2 tbsp
baby sweetcorn	125 g/5 oz
Thai green curry paste	30 ml/2 tbsp
can of coconut milk	1 large
can of sliced bamboo shoots	1 small, drained
boiled rice or noodles and chilli sauce	to serve

1 Fry the chicken fillets in half the oil over a moderately high heat for 4 minutes, turning until lightly browned. Remove and set aside.

2 Stir-fry the sweetcorn in the rest of the oil for 3 minutes.

3 Add the curry paste and cook for 1 minute, stirring all the time.

4 Gradually stir in the coconut milk and bring to the boil. Stir in the chicken and bamboo shoots.

5 Lower the heat and simmer for 5 minutes until the chicken and sweetcorn are tender and cooked through.

6 Serve with rice or noodles and chilli sauce, if liked.

creamy chicken korma

You can adapt the recipe using any curry paste if you prefer a different spice combination.

SERVES 2
READY IN **30 MINUTES**

ingredients	quantity and preparation
skinless, boneless chicken breasts	2
cornflour (cornstarch)	5 ml/1 tsp
thick plain yoghurt	150 ml/¼ pt/⅔ cup
onion	1
oil	15 ml/1 tbsp
garlic purée (paste)	5 ml/1 tsp
korma curry paste	15 ml/1 tbsp
hot chicken or vegetable stock	120 ml/4 fl oz/½ cup
salt and freshly ground black pepper	
basmati rice, peas and popadoms	to serve

1 Cut each chicken breast into 3 chunks.

2 Blend the cornflour with 15 ml/1 tbsp of the yoghurt, then stir in the rest of the yoghurt.

3 Fry the onion in the oil for 7 minutes, stirring occasionally until soft.

4 Stir in the garlic and curry paste and cook for 1 minute, stirring.

5 Stir in the stock, salt and pepper. Add the chicken, half-cover and simmer gently for 10 minutes.

6 On the lowest heat, stir in the yogurt mixture a spoonful at a time. Simmer for 5 minutes or until the chicken is cooked through.

7 Serve with rice, peas and popadoms

honey-glazed chicken

Loads of flavour, yet very easy, this has a delicious sweet glaze. You can cook it on the barbecue if you like.

SERVES 2
READY IN **30 MINUTES**

ingredients	quantity and preparation
boneless, skinless chicken breasts	2
salt and freshly ground black pepper	
honey	30 ml/2 tbsp
tomato ketchup (catsup)	30 ml/2 tbsp
orange juice	30 ml/2 tbsp
new potatoes and a green vegetable	to serve

1 Turn on the oven to 180°C/350°F/gas 4.

2 Season the chicken breasts to taste with salt and pepper, then arrange snugly in a small roasting tin.

3 Mix the honey, ketchup and orange juice in a small bowl and pour over the chicken.

4 Bake in the oven for 20 minutes or until the chicken is cooked through.

5 Slice the chicken on the diagonal and serve with new potatoes and a green vegetable such as courgettes.

creamy mushroom chicken

Cooked in one pan, condensed soup makes an easy sauce that is especially good with chicken.

SERVES 2
READY IN **30 MINUTES**

ingredients	quantity and preparation
skinless, boneless chicken breasts	2, sliced
oil	15 ml/1 tbsp
button mushrooms	50 g/2 oz, halved if large
can of condensed cream of mushroom soup	1 small
milk	120 ml/4 fl oz/½ cup
black pepper	to serve
buttered noodles	
dried mixed herbs	2.5 ml/½ tsp

1 Fry the chicken in the oil for 5 minutes over a moderate heat, turning. Add the mushrooms and fry for 5 minutes, turning occasionally. Stir in the soup, milk and pepper and simmer gently for 10 minutes.

2 Serve with buttered noodles.

turkey

Turkey makes great comfort food. It has a stronger flavour than chicken but one that still goes well with all kinds of sauces, creamy or rich and flavoursome. You can use it in the chicken recipes too, for more variety, but you may need to cook them for a little longer.

It's worth keeping some turkey strips or escalopes in the freezer, for when you need them.

stir-fry turkey with noodles

A delicious all-in-one, Chinese-style dish, this is easy to put together when you get home from work.

SERVES 2
READY IN **15 MINUTES**

ingredients	quantity and preparation
clear honey	10 ml/2 tsp
dark soy sauce	15–30 ml/1–2 tbsp
lemon juice or wine vinegar	5 ml/1 tsp
bottled grated ginger	10 ml/2 tsp
turkey strips	225 g/8 oz
dried flat rice noodles	175 g/6 oz
oil	30 ml/2 tbsp
mixed stir-fry vegetables	350 g/12 oz pack
cornflour (cornstarch)	5 ml/1 tsp
hot chicken or vegetable stock or water	120 ml/4 fl oz/½ cup

1 Mix together the honey, soy sauce, lemon juice or vinegar and ginger in a bowl. Add the turkey and toss to coat. Leave to marinate for a few minutes.

2 Put the noodles in a heatproof bowl and pour boiling water over. Soak for 3 minutes, then drain.

3 Meanwhile, heat half the oil in a frying pan. Lift the turkey out of the marinade, add to the pan and stir-fry over a high heat for 4 minutes. Remove and return to the marinade.

4 Stir-fry the vegetables in the remaining oil for 4 minutes over a medium-high heat.

5 Blend the cornflour with a little cold water, then add the stock or water. Add to the pan with the chicken and marinade and bring to the boil, stirring.

6 Cook for a minute more, then add the noodles and stir-fry for 2 minutes until piping hot.

turkey satay sticks

Try making this easy dish with chicken
or with ready-cut turkey strips if you
are short of time.

SERVES 2
READY IN **30 MINUTES**

ingredients	quantity and preparation
turkey breast steaks	2
oil	10 ml/2 tsp
soy sauce	15 ml/1 tbsp
lemon juice	5 ml/1 tsp
For the peanut sauce	
onion	1, finely chopped
oil	15 ml/1 tbsp
garlic purée (paste)	5 ml/1 tsp
chilli powder **or dried chilli flakes**	¼ tsp a pinch
water	15 ml/1 tbsp
peanut butter	30 ml/2 tbsp
sugar	5 ml/1 tsp
lemon juice	5 ml/1 tsp
egg noodles	125 g/5 oz, to serve

1 Cut the turkey into strips.

2 Put the oil, soy sauce and lemon juice in a bowl and whisk together with a fork. Add the turkey and stir to coat. Leave to marinate for a few minutes.

3 Fry the onion in the oil for 7 minutes until soft, stirring often.

4 Add the garlic and chilli and cook for 1 minute, stirring. Turn off the heat.

5 Stir in the water, peanut butter, sugar and lemon juice.

6 Line a grill (broiler) pan with foil (to save on washing up) and heat the grill to medium high. Thread the turkey strips concertina-style on to 4 skewers (soak them in water first if using wooden ones).

7 Cook the skewers under the grill for 5 minutes, turning them a few times, until cooked through.

8 While the turkey is cooking, cook the noodles in boiling water for 3 minutes, following the packet instructions. Drain well.

9 Heat the peanut sauce until hot and serve with the turkey skewers and noodles.

pan-fried turkey escalopes

Put the oven on and get the chips in the oven before you start cooking as this is a really quick dish.

SERVES 2
READY IN **20 MINUTES**

ingredients	quantity and preparation
egg	1, lightly beaten
plain (all-purpose) flour	30 ml/2 tbsp
salt and pepper	
oil	15 ml/1 tbsp
unsalted butter	30 ml/2 tbsp
turkey escalopes	2
oven chips and peas	to serve

1 Put the egg in a bowl and the flour in another. Season the flour with salt and pepper. Heat the oil and butter in a frying pan.

2 Dip the turkey in the egg, then in the flour and fry until golden on both sides, then reduce the heat and fry until cooked through.

3 Serve with chips and peas.

fish and seafood

The best way to cook fish is fast, making it ideal
for super-quick suppers when you need something
comforting and hot after a long day at work. It's also
good for you and contains oils that are beneficial for
both your heart and your brain. Don't let the thought of
preparation put you off; all the recipes here use ready-
prepared fish and there are also plenty of ideas for
making the most of canned fish as well.

When buying fish, if it's really fresh it shouldn't smell too
'fishy'. Buy from a reliable source and make sure that it
looks firm and moist. Both fresh and frozen fish should
be put in the fridge or freezer as soon as possible and,
ideally, fresh fish should be eaten on the day you buy it.

fish and vegetable parcels

Cooking fish in greaseproof paper parcels keeps in all the flavour. Try this with salmon for a change.

SERVES 2
READY IN **30 MINUTES**

ingredients	quantity and preparation
white fish, such as sustainable cod	2 pieces, about 100 g/4 oz each
lemon juice	10 ml/2 tsp
salt and freshly ground black pepper	
carrot	1, cut into matchstick strips
baby leek	1, very thinly sliced
button mushrooms	50 g/2 oz, sliced
new potatoes	to serve

1 Turn on the oven to 180°C/350°F/gas 4.

2 Cut out two dinner-plate-sized circles from baking parchment or greaseproof paper.

3 Place a piece of fish on one half of each circle and sprinkle each with 5 ml/1 tsp of the lemon juice, then season with salt and pepper. Scatter the carrot, leek and mushrooms over the fish.

4 Fold over the top half of the circle to make a semi-circle, then seal the edges of the parcels by turning and pleating the edges of the paper.

5 Place on a baking tray and bake in the oven for 15 minutes.

6 Snip a hole in the top of each parcel to let out some of the hot steam before serving with new potatoes.

tasty tuna fishcakes

Look out for canned tuna on special offer – it's a useful standby to keep in the cupboard.

SERVES 2
READY IN **40 MINUTES**

ingredients	quantity and preparation
potatoes	2, diced
pesto	30 ml/2 tbsp
can of tuna fish, drained	1 small
egg	1, lightly beaten
salt and freshly ground black pepper	
plain (all-purpose) flour	15 ml/1 tbsp
fine polenta	60 ml/4 tbsp
oil	30 ml/2 tbsp
sweetcorn and peas and lemon mayonnaise	to serve

1 Cook the potatoes in boiling lightly salted water for 15 minutes or until tender. Drain and mash with the pesto. Cool for 10 minutes.

2 Stir the tuna into the potato with 15 ml/1 tbsp of the beaten egg, some salt and pepper.

3 With lightly floured hands, shape the tuna mixture into 4 fishcakes, each about 2.5 cm/ 1 in thick.

4 Dip each fishcake into the remaining beaten egg, then into the polenta to coat.

5 Fry the fishcakes in hot oil over a moderate heat for 3 minutes on each side until golden.

6 Serve with sweetcorn and peas and some mayonnaise spiced with a dash of lemon juice.

citrus salmon with stir-fried vegetables

Salmon steaks are low fat, high protein and very tasty, but this works well with hake or haddock too.

SERVES 2
READY IN **25 MINUTES**

ingredients	quantity and preparation
skinned salmon steaks	2
oil	30 ml/2 tbsp
lemon juice	10 ml/2 tsp
salt and freshly ground black pepper	
stir-fried vegetables	300 g/11 oz packet
soy sauce	15 ml/1 tbsp
clear honey	10 ml/2 tsp
orange juice	30 ml/2 tbsp

1 Preheat the grill (broiler) to moderate and line the grill pan with foil. Place the fish on the grill rack, with the underside uppermost.

2 Mix 15 ml/1 tbsp of the oil, the lemon juice and salt and pepper and drizzle half over the fish.

3 Grill for 4 minutes, then turn over, drizzle with the rest of the lemon mixture and cook for 3 minutes or until the fish is cooked through.

4 While the fish is grilling, heat the remaining oil in a non-stick frying pan. Add the vegetables and stir-fry for 3 minutes.

5 Add the soy sauce, honey and orange juice. Stir-fry for 2 minutes or until the vegetables are tender.

6 Spoon the vegetables on to plates and serve the fish on top.

creamy fish pie

Vary the quantities and varieties of fish to ring the changes in this homely fish pie.

SERVES 2
READY IN **60 MINUTES**

ingredients	quantity and preparation
potatoes	2, cut into chunks
butter	about 15 ml/1 tbsp
milk	15 ml/1 tbsp
salt and freshly ground black pepper	
skinless, boneless white fish such as sustainable cod or haddock	175 g/6 oz piece
raw peeled prawns	100 g/4 oz
frozen peas or mixed vegetables	50 g/2 oz
cream cheese	150 g/5 oz

1 Cook the potatoes in boiling water for
15 minutes until tender. Drain and mash with
the butter, milk, salt and pepper.

2 Turn on the oven to 180°C/350°F/gas 4. Cut
the fish into chunks and put in an ovenproof
dish with the prawns and peas or mixed
vegetables. Season with salt and pepper.

3 Give the cream cheese a stir to soften it, then
dot small spoonfuls all over the fish and prawns
(this will combine with the fish juices as it cooks
to make a sauce).

4 Top with the mashed potato and bake for
30 minutes. Check that that the fish is white
and the prawns completely pink (this shows
that they are cooked) before serving.

seafood paella

This is a very simple version of this classic dish. Use a packet of cooked prawns if you prefer.

SERVES 2
READY IN **30 MINUTES**

ingredients	quantity and preparation
onion	1, sliced
oil	15 ml/1 tbsp
garlic purée (paste)	5 ml/1 tsp
red (bell) pepper or frozen sliced peppers	1, sliced
	50 g/2 oz
ground turmeric	a large pinch
dried mixed herbs	a large pinch
long-grain rice	100 g/4 oz/½ cup
hot vegetable stock	450 ml/¾ pt/2 cups
can of chopped tomatoes	1 small
mixed cooked seafood, thawed if frozen	200 g/7 oz packet

1 Fry the onion in the oil in a non-stick frying pan for 5 minutes, stirring often.

2 Add the garlic and cook for 1 minute.

3 Sir in the pepper slices, turmeric, herbs and rice.

4 Add the stock and tomatoes. Stir and bring to the boil.

5 Turn down the heat to low and simmer for 15 minutes or until the rice is just tender, stirring once or twice during cooking.

6 Stir in the seafood and season with salt and pepper. Cook for 2 minutes until piping hot.

prawn and cashew stir-fry

When you are stir-frying, make sure you prepare all the ingredients before starting to cook.

SERVES 2
READY IN **15 MINUTES**

ingredients	quantity and preparation
oil	15 ml/1 tbsp
sugar snap peas or mangetout	50 g/2 oz
garlic purée (paste)	5 ml/1 tsp
ginger purée (paste)	5 ml/1 tsp
unsalted cashew nuts	100 g/4 oz
cooked, peeled prawns	100 g/4 oz
soy sauce	15 ml/1 tbsp
orange juice	15 ml/1 tbsp
honey	5 ml/1 tsp
quick-cook noodles	to serve

1 Heat the oil in a wok or large frying pan. Add the sugar snap peas or mangetout and stir-fry for 2 minutes.

2 Add the garlic, ginger and nuts and stir-fry for 2 minutes or until the nuts start to brown.

3 Stir in the prawns, soy sauce, orange juice and honey. Stir-fry for 2 minutes or until everything is hot and coated in the sauce.

4 Serve with noodles.

thai crab cakes

Mix a little garlic purée into your mayonnaise for extra flavour in this Oriental-style dish.

SERVES 2
READY IN **20 MINUTES**

ingredients	quantity and preparation
can of white crabmeat in brine	1 small
mayonnaise	45 ml/3 tbsp
lemon juice	10 ml/2 tsp
freshly ground black pepper	
dried chilli flakes or chilli powder	a small pinch
spring onions (scallions)	3, thinly sliced
egg	1
natural breadcrumbs	50 g/2 oz
oil	30 ml/2 tbsp
sweet chilli dipping sauce and a baby leaf or oriental salad	to serve

1 Tip the crabmeat into a sieve over the sink and leave to drain.

2 Mix the mayonnaise, lemon juice, pepper, chilli and spring onions in a bowl.

3 Press down on the crabmeat with the back of a spoon to squeeze out as much liquid as possible. Tip the crabmeat into the bowl and mix everything together well.

4 Shape the mixture into 6 small crab cakes.

5 Lightly beat the egg on a plate and tip the breadcrumbs on to a second plate.

6 Dip each crab cake first into the beaten egg, then into breadcrumbs to coat.

7 Shallow-fry in hot oil over a moderate heat for 2 minutes on each side until lightly browned. Serve with sweet chilli dipping sauce and a baby leaf or oriental-style salad.

spicy seafood pasta

Add a teaspoon of garlic purée or
a crushed clove of garlic with the
onions if you like a garlic flavour.

SERVES 2
READY IN **15 MINUTES**

ingredients	quantity and preparation
large pasta shapes	400 g/14 oz/4 cups
spring onions	6, sliced
oil	10 ml/2 tsp
chopped tomatoes	1 small can
mild chilli powder	2.5 ml/½ tsp
mixed seafood	200 g/7 oz, thawed if frozen
salt and pepper	

1 Cook the pasta in boiling salted water for
10 minutes.

2 Cook the onions in the oil for 3 minutes,
stirring. Stir in the tomatoes and chilli and
simmer for 4 minutes.

3 Stir in the seafood, season and simmer for a
few minutes until cooked.

4 Drain the pasta, toss together and serve.

vegetarian

Even the most hardened carnivore will enjoy these meat- and fish-free meals. The recipes do include dairy products so vegetarians will need to read the labels on cheeses and so on to check whether they are suitable. Look out, too, for vegetarian versions of products like Worcestershire sauce.

Vegetarians are good at making sure they get plenty of vitamins and minerals in their diet, from nuts, pulses, dried fruit such as apricots and fortified breakfast cereals. Eating or drinking vitamin-C-rich foods, such as a glass of orange juice, with a meal will help your body to absorb all-important iron.

spicy vegetable and pasta bake

Pasta bakes are great comfort food and this is a tasty vegetable-based option.

SERVES 2
READY IN **35 MINUTES**

ingredients	quantity and preparation
dried pasta shapes	225 g/8 oz/2 cups
onion	1, chopped
oil	15 ml/1 tbsp
mushrooms	50 g/2 oz, sliced
courgettes (zucchini)	2, sliced
red (bell) pepper	½, sliced
or frozen sliced mixed peppers	50 g/2 oz
garlic purée (paste)	5 ml/1 tsp
dried mixed herbs	5 ml/1 tsp
vegetarian Worcestershire sauce	5 ml/1 tsp
can of condensed cream of tomato soup	1 small
Cheddar cheese	50 g/2 oz, grated

1 Turn on the oven to 200°C/400°F/gas 6.

2 Cook the pasta in salted boiling water for 9 minutes or for 1 minute less than the packet instructions, until almost tender. Drain and tip back into the pan.

3 Meanwhile, fry the onion in the oil over a medium heat for 8 minutes, stirring.

4 Add the mushrooms and courgettes and cook, stirring frequently, for 2 minutes.

5 Add the pepper slices and garlic and cook for 1 minute, stirring.

6 Stir in the herbs, Worcestershire sauce and tomato soup. Bring to the boil.

7 Add to the pasta and mix well, then tip into an ovenproof dish. Scatter the cheese over the top and bake in the oven for 20 minutes.

vegetable crumble

Crumble doesn't have to be apple!
Here is delicious proof that crumbles
don't have to be sweet.

SERVES 2
READY IN **50 MINUTES**

ingredients	quantity and preparation
For the topping	
wholemeal or plain (all-purpose) flour	100 g/4 oz/1 cup
butter or margarine	50 g/2 oz/¼ mug, cubed
vegetarian cheese	50 g/2 oz, grated
almonds, walnuts or cashew nuts	50 g/2 oz, roughly chopped
For the filling	
butter or margarine	about 30 ml/2 tbsp
leek	1, sliced
carrot	1, sliced
baby mushrooms	50 g/2 oz
sweet potato	1, cubed
plain (all-purpose) flour	15 ml/1 tbsp
vegetable stock	150 ml/¼ pt/⅔ cup
salt and pepper	
mascarpone cheese	75 g/3 oz

1 Turn on the oven to 180°C/350°F/gas 4.

2 For the topping, put the flour and butter in a bowl. Rub in the butter with your fingertips until the mixture looks like breadcrumbs. Stir in the grated cheese and nuts.

3 For the filling, melt the butter in a saucepan. Add the leek and stir to coat, then cover the pan with a lid and cook gently for 3 minutes.

4 Add the carrot, mushrooms and sweet potato and fry, stirring often, for 5 minutes.

5 Sprinkle over the flour and stir in, then gradually add the stock and season with salt and pepper. Simmer for 1 minute, then stir in the mascarpone cheese.

6 Tip the mixture into a shallow ovenproof dish and sprinkle over the crumble topping. Bake in the oven for 30 minutes or until lightly browned.

filo-topped vegetable pie

Wrap tightly in clingfilm (plastic wrap) and chill or freeze the rest of the filo pastry for use in another dish.

SERVES 2
READY IN **30 MINUTES**

ingredients	quantity and preparation
cornflour (cornstarch)	30 ml/2 tbsp
milk	250 ml/8 fl oz/1 cup
dried mixed herbs	2.5 ml/½ tsp
vegetable stock cube	½
vegetarian Cheddar cheese	50 g/2 oz
frozen mixed vegetables such as cauliflower, carrots and peas	250 g/9 oz, thawed
salt and freshly ground black pepper	
filo pastry	4 sheets
oil	30 ml/2 tbsp

1 Mix the cornflour with 30 ml/2 tbsp of the milk in a small saucepan. Stir in the rest of the milk, add the herbs and crumble in the stock cube. Bring to the boil, stirring until the sauce has thickened.

2 Turn off the heat and stir the cheese and vegetables into the sauce. Season with salt and pepper. Tip into an ovenproof dish. Turn on the oven to 200°C/400°F/gas 6.

3 Roughly cut each sheet of filo pastry into four rectangles. Brush each with a little of the oil, then scrunch up slightly and put on top of the vegetable mixture.

4 Bake in the oven for 20 minutes, or until the vegetables are tender and the pastry golden and crispy.

potato and pea frittata

Cook extra potatoes when you are cooking the night before to use in this frittata.

SERVES 2
READY IN **30 MINUTES**

ingredients	quantity and preparation
onion	1, chopped
oil	15–30 ml/1–2 tbsp
garlic purée (paste)	5 ml/1 tsp
cooked potatoes	2, diced
frozen peas, thawed	175 g/6 oz
eggs	4
milk	30 ml/2 tbsp
dried mixed herbs	2.5 ml/½ tsp
salt and freshly ground black pepper	
vegetarian Cheddar cheese	50 g/2 oz, grated

1 Gently fry the onion in the oil for 8 minutes, stirring frequently, until almost soft.

2 Turn the heat up a little, add the garlic and diced potatoes and stir-fry for 1 minute.

3 Stir in the peas and spread out to an even layer on the base of the pan. Turn down the heat to low.

4 Whisk the eggs, milk, herbs, salt and pepper together in a jug. Pour over the vegetables.

5 Cook for 10 minutes, or until the base of the frittata is set and lightly browned.

6 Scatter the cheese over the top, then place under a medium grill (broiler) for 4 minutes or until the top is set and golden brown.

7 Leave to settle and cool in the pan for a couple of minutes before cutting into thick wedges.

cheese and courgette tart

If you have to buy a large packet, chill or freeze the rest of the pastry to use on another day.

SERVES 2
READY IN **60 MINUTES**

ingredients	quantity and preparation
ready-rolled puff pastry	200 g/7 oz
milk	15 ml/1 tbsp
onion	1, sliced
oil	15–30 ml/1–2 tbsp
courgette (zucchini)	1, sliced
dried mixed herbs	2.5 ml/½ tsp
salt and freshly ground black pepper	
cherry tomatoes	6, halved
mozzarella cheese	150 g/5 oz packet, diced
mixed salad	to serve

1 Unroll the pastry and put it on a baking tray. Brush the milk around the edge to make a 1 cm border.

2 Fry the onion in the oil in a frying pan for 7 minutes, stirring now and then until beginning to soften.

3 Stir in the courgette and cook for 3 minutes, stirring frequently.

4 Stir in the herbs and salt and pepper, then cool for a few minutes while preparing the rest of the ingredients. Turn on the oven to 220°C/425°F/gas 7.

5 Spoon the onion mixture over the pastry, but do not cover the milk-brushed border.

6 Arrange the tomatoes, cut-side upwards, on top, then scatter with the cheese.

7 Bake in the oven for 30 minutes, or until the pastry is well risen and golden.

8 Serve with a mixed salad.

cheese and bread pudding

This is a great way to use up slightly stale bread and makes a simple and warming supper.

SERVES 2
READY IN **45 MINUTES**

ingredients	quantity and preparation
butter or margarine	15 ml/1 tbsp
stale white bread	5 slices, cut into triangles
vegetarian cheese	100 g/4 oz/1 cup, grated
eggs	3
milk	450 ml/¾ pt/2 cups
mild mustard	½ tsp
salt and pepper	
tomatoes	2, sliced

1 Turn on the oven to 200°C/400°F/gas 6 and grease a shallow ovenproof dish. Arrange the bread in the dish. Scatter over the cheese. Whisk the eggs, milk, mustard, salt and pepper, pour over to coat the bread and cheese, and leave to soak for 5 minutes.

2 Arrange the tomatoes on top. Bake for 30 minutes until golden brown and lightly set.

quick snacks

Especially if you are not too confident in the kitchen, this chapter is a good place to start to find some quick and easy recipes when you have little time and perhaps want something to keep you going until your proper meal, or just a light meal or snack.

And for those of you on a budget, mastering these will bring big savings compared with takeaways and sandwich shops.

salmon-stuffed jacket potatoes

Jacket potatoes are quickest cooked in the microwave and make a versatile snack or the basis of a simple meal.

SERVES 2
READY IN **15 MINUTES (MICROWAVE)**

ingredients	quantity and preparation
baking potatoes	2, scrubbed
oil	
salt and freshly ground black pepper	
cream cheese	100 g/4 oz/½ cup
Greek-style yoghurt	60 ml/4 tbsp
can of pink salmon	1 small, flaked
butter or margarine	15 ml/1 tbsp

1 Prick the potatoes all over with a fork (this is essential to stop them exploding!). Microwave on High for 5 minutes.

2 Rub the skin with a little oil and salt. Microwave on High for a further 3 minutes or until the potatoes feel soft when gently squeezed. Leave to 'rest' for a minute.

3 Or to oven bake, heat your oven to 180°C/350°F/gas 4. Prick the potatoes, rub with oil and salt and bake for 1¼ hours or until tender.

4 Mix the cream cheese with 30 ml/2 tbsp of the yoghurt. Gently stir in the salmon.

5 Halve the potatoes lengthways. Scoop out the flesh and mash in a bowl with the butter or margarine and the rest of the yoghurt, salt and pepper.

6 Pile the mixture back into the potato skins and spoon the salmon mixture on top.

one-pot chicken noodles

With no artificial colours or flavourings and made from fresh ingredients, this is far superior to those store brands.

SERVES 2
READY IN **20 MINUTES**

ingredients	quantity and preparation
oil	15 ml/1 tbsp
skinless, boneless chicken breasts	2, cut into chunks
spring onions (scallions)	4, sliced
red or yellow (bell) pepper	1, sliced
garlic clove	1, crushed
chicken or vegetable stock cube	½
boiling water	250 ml/8 fl oz/1 cup
sugar	a pinch
soy sauce	15 ml/1 tbsp
fine egg noodles	100 g/4 oz

1 Heat the oil in a large pan or wok. Add the chicken and spring onions and stir-fry for 3 minutes.

2 Add the pepper and garlic and stir-fry for 1 minute.

3 Crumble over the stock cube and add the boiling water, sugar and soy sauce. When the mixture boils, turn down the heat, cover and cook for 2 minutes.

4 Break the blocks of noodles into smaller pieces. Add to the pan and stir. Cover and cook for 3 minutes. Serve straight away.

easy egg-fried rice

If you don't have leftover rice, you'll need about 175 g/6 oz/¾ cup of uncooked rice to make this quantity.

SERVES 2
READY IN **15 MINUTES**

ingredients	quantity and preparation
oil	15 ml/1 tbsp
green or red (bell) pepper	1, chopped
frozen peas	30 ml/2 tbsp
frozen sweetcorn	30 ml/2 tbsp
egg	1
cold water	15 ml/1 tbsp
cooked long-grain rice	275 g/10 oz/2½ cups
soy sauce	15 ml/1 tbsp

1 Heat the oil in a wok or non-stick frying pan. Add the pepper and stir-fry for 2 minutes.

2 Add the peas and sweetcorn and heat through.

3 Beat together the egg and water, then stir into the pan. Leave to cook for 30 seconds, then stir to break up the egg.

4 Add the rice and soy sauce and stir-fry for 2 minutes or until heated through.

potato wedges and cheese dip

These are great for munching while watching TV – but watch out, they are very moreish!

SERVES 2
READY IN **40 MINUTES**

ingredients	quantity and preparation
oil	15–30 ml/1–2 tbsp
potatoes	4, scrubbed
salt and freshly ground black pepper	
mustard	2.5 ml/½ tsp
tomato purée (paste)	5 ml/1 tsp
soured cream	150 ml/¼ pt/⅔ cup
Cheddar cheese	50 g/2 oz/½ cup, grated
a few carrot or celery sticks or sliced red (bell) pepper	to serve

1 Turn on the oven to 200°C/400°F/gas 6.

2 Pour the oil on to a non-stick baking tray and put in the oven to heat.

3 Cut the potatoes in half lengthways, then cut each half into thick wedges. Put in a saucepan, pour over enough boiling water to cover and bring back to the boil. Season with salt. Cover and simmer for 3 minutes. Drain.

4 Tip on to the baking sheet and turn to coat in the oil. Bake for 25 minutes or until dark golden brown, turning over half-way through.

5 For the dip, mix together the mustard, tomato purée and a spoonful of the soured cream. Stir in the rest of the cream and cheese and season with salt and pepper.

6 Serve the dip with the potato wedges and a few fresh vegetable sticks.

nachos

Perfect for a fast and fun snack, you can use plain corn chips or tortilla chips, if you prefer.

SERVES 2
READY IN **10 MINUTES**

ingredients	quantity and preparation
plain corn chips	1 small packet
Cheddar cheese	100 g/4 oz/1 cup, grated
spicy tomato salsa	1 medium jar

1 Turn on the oven to 220°C/425°F/gas 7.

2 Pile the chips in a shallow ovenproof dish.

3 Sprinkle the cheese all over the chips.

4 Bake in the oven for 3 minutes until the cheese is melted but not browned.

5 Drizzle the salsa over the top and eat straight away.

sweet stuff

Desserts are the ultimate comfort food, so even if you don't indulge often – and we all know they are meant as an occasional treat – there are times when nothing but chocolate cake will give you the right degree of comfort!

If you have a go at making a cake or two, do take the trouble to line your tins with baking parchment. The easiest way is to use ready-shaped cake-tin or loaf-tin liners – or you can use the latest flexible silicone 'tins'.

gooey chocolate pudding

This pudding should have a crisp crust and a squidgy middle, so don't overcook it!

SERVES 2
READY IN **45 MINUTES**

ingredients	quantity and preparation
butter or margarine, at room temperature, plus extra for greasing	50 g/2 oz/¼ cup
plain (semi-sweet) chocolate or packet of plain chocolate chips	100 g/4 oz
light soft brown sugar	175 g/3 oz/⅓ cup
eggs	2, lightly beaten
self-raising flour	50 g/2 oz/¼ cup
ice-cream or single (light) cream	to serve

1 Turn on the oven to 190°C/375°F/gas 5. Grease an ovenproof dish.

2 Put the chocolate in a bowl and carefully put the bowl in a pan of boiling water (it should reach about half-way up the bowl). Leave for 3 minutes, then stir until melted. Take the bowl out of the hot water.

3 Beat the butter or margarine and sugar together until creamy, then beat in the eggs a little at a time.

4 Stir in the melted chocolate. Tip in the flour and stir in with a metal spoon.

5 Pour into the greased dish and cook for 30 minutes. Serve hot with ice-cream or cream.

crunchy oat fruit crumble

For variety, you can make this with canned peaches, apricots, pears or plums or a can of fruit filling.

SERVES 2
READY IN **40 MINUTES**

ingredients	quantity and preparation
can of fruit in syrup	1 large
plain (all-purpose) flour	50 g/2 oz/½ cup
rolled porridge oats	50 g/2 oz/½ cup
light soft brown sugar	50 g/2 oz/¼ cup
butter or margarine	50 g/2 oz/¼ cup
custard or ice-cream	to serve

1 Turn on the oven to 190°C/375°F/gas 5.

2 Spoon the fruit into an ovenproof dish, then add about 4 tablespoons of the syrup (resist any temptation to add more or the crumble will be soggy).

3 Put the flour, oats and sugar in a mixing bowl. Cut the butter or margarine into small pieces and rub in.

4 Sprinkle the crumble topping evenly over the fruit.

5 Bake in the oven for 25 minutes, or until the top is well browned and crisp.

6 Serve with custard or ice-cream.

golden double syrup pudding

This light, fluffy sponge is just drenched in syrup and crying out for hot, fresh custard!

SERVES 2
READY IN **20 MINUTES (MICROWAVE)**

ingredients	quantity and preparation
golden (light corn) syrup	90 ml/6 tbsp
plain (all-purpose) flour	100 g/4 oz/1 cup
baking powder	12.5 ml/2½ tsp
salt	a pinch
butter or margarine	100 g/4 oz/½ cup
soft brown sugar	100 g/4 oz/½ cup
eggs	2, lightly beaten
custard	to serve

1 Grease a large pudding bowl.

2 Put 30 ml/2 tbsp of the syrup in the bottom of the bowl.

3 Beat the flour, baking powder, salt, butter or margarine, sugar and eggs for several minutes until well blended. Spoon into the bowl.

4 To steam: cover securely with greased kitchen foil, place in a large pan and fill with boiling water to come half way up the basin. Cover and boil for 1½ hours, topping up with boiling water as necessary.

5 Alternatively, to microwave: cover with baking parchment or a lid and microwave for 4 minutes. Leave to stand for 1 minute, then test the pudding to see if a knife comes out clean from the centre. If not, microwave in 1-minute bursts, resting between each one.

6 Warm the remaining syrup. When the pudding is ready, turn it out on to a deep serving dish and pierce several times with a skewer. Pour over the syrup.

7 Serve with plenty of hot custard.

chocolate cream cake

Perfect when you need a chocolate fix, this is delicious for tea time, with coffee or as a dessert.

MAKES 1
READY IN **50 MINUTES**

ingredients	quantity and preparation
plain (all-purpose) flour	200 g/7 oz/1¾ cups
cocoa (unsweetened chocolate) powder	30 ml/2 tbsp
bicarbonate of soda (baking soda)	5 ml/1 tsp
baking powder	5 ml/1 tsp
caster (superfine) sugar	150 g/5 oz/⅔ cup
golden (light corn) syrup	30 ml/2 tbsp
eggs	2, lightly beaten
oil	150 ml/¼ pt/⅔ cup
milk	150 ml/¼ pt/⅔ cup
double (heavy) cream	150 ml/¼ pt/⅔ cup
icing (confectioners') sugar	15 ml/1 tbsp

1 Turn on the oven to 160°C/325°F/gas 3. Grease and line two 20 cm/8 in cake tins (pans).

2 Mix all the dry ingredients in a bowl.

3 Add the syrup, eggs, oil and milk and mix to a batter – the mixture will be thinner than most cake mixes.

4 Divide between the prepared cake tins.

5 Bake in the oven for 35 minutes or until well risen and springy to the touch. Turn on to a wire rack to cool.

6 Whisk the cream until stiff and use to sandwich the two cakes together. Sprinkle with icing sugar to serve.

chocolate chip cookies

This has to be everyone's favourite biscuit and is an absolute must in a book on comfort food.

MAKES 20
READY IN **25 MINUTES**

ingredients	quantity and preparation
butter or margarine, at room temperature	75 g/3 oz/⅓ cup
light soft brown sugar	50 g/2 oz/¼ cup
egg	1, lightly beaten
golden (light corn) syrup	45 ml/3 tbsp
self-raising flour	175 g/6 oz/1½ cups
bicarbonate of soda (baking soda)	a pinch
chocolate chips	100 g/4 oz/1 cup

1 Turn on the oven to 190°C/375°F/gas 5.

2 Beat the butter or margarine and sugar together in a bowl until creamy. Add the beaten egg, then add the syrup, flour, bicarbonate of soda and chocolate chips. Stir everything together to make a thick dough.

3 With floured hands, roll pieces of the dough into balls about the size of a walnut. Put on lightly greased (or baking parchment lined) baking sheets, spacing them slightly apart, and flatten them a little.

4 Bake in the oven for 10–15 minutes until golden brown.

5 Lift on to a wire rack. When cool, store in an airtight container – they will keep for up to a week.

blueberry and white chocolate muffins

You can turn these into any kind of muffins by changing what you add to the basic mixture.

MAKES 12
READY IN **30 MINUTES**

ingredients	quantity and preparation
plain (all-purpose) flour	225 g/8 oz/2 cups
baking powder	5 ml/1 tsp
caster (superfine) sugar	100 g/4 oz/½ cup
salt	a pinch
egg	1, lightly beaten
milk	250 ml/8 fl oz/1 cup
sunflower oil	120 ml/4 fl oz/½ cup
fresh blueberries	225 g/8 oz
white chocolate chips	225 g/8 oz/2 cups

1 Turn on the oven to 200°C/400°F/gas 6 and put muffin cases in a muffin tin.

2 Mix the flour, baking powder, sugar and salt in a bowl, then make a hole in the centre.

3 Add the egg, milk and oil into the hole and stir round decisively once or twice so they are beginning to mix together.

4 Add the blueberries and chocolate chips and fold the ingredients together until they are just blended. Do not overmix.

5 Spoon into the prepared cases and bake in the oven for 20 minutes until golden and springy to the touch.

index